Three Minutes a Day

VOLUME 48

THREE MINUTES A DAY
VOLUME 48

Tony Rossi
Editor-in-Chief

Gerald M. Costello
Contributing Editor

The Christophers
5 Hanover Square
New York, NY 10004

www.christophers.org

Lord, make me an instrument of Your peace.
Where there is hatred, let me sow love;
where there is injury, pardon;
where there is doubt, faith;
where there is despair, hope;
where there is darkness, light;
and where there is sadness, joy.

O Divine Master, grant that I may not so much seek
to be consoled as to console;
to be understood as to understand;
to be loved as to love.
For it is in giving that we receive;
it is in pardoning that we are pardoned;
and it is in dying that we are born to eternal life.
Amen.

PRAYER OF ST. FRANCIS
(ADOPTED AS THE PRAYER OF THE CHRISTOPHERS)

The Christophers warmly thank
all our friends, sponsors and supporters
who have made this 48th volume of
Three Minutes a Day possible.

Contributing Writers

Tony Rossi

Gerald M. Costello

Sarah E. Holinski

Joan Bromfield

Monica Ann Yehle Glick

Julie Baldwin

Dear Christopher Friends,

We are pleased to present Volume 48 of our *Three Minutes a Day* book. This series of publications is beloved by people throughout the world, and we encourage all who enjoy our daily inspirational messages to spread the word about our mission, which is summarized in our motto and the ancient Chinese proverb, "It's better to light one candle than to curse the darkness."

Contained within the pages of this book are short readings that highlight real-life stories that affirm the highest values of the human spirit. We hope readers will be inspired to recognize the good that exists in others and to seek out opportunities to make a positive difference in the world.

Our founder, Father James Keller, M.M., taught that each person has a unique purpose in life, and encouraged all people to realize the importance of using their talents for the greater good because even the smallest act of kindness can help to bring about a miracle.

We hope *Three Minutes a Day* serves as a catalyst for those who open this book to embrace the talents God has given them so they can achieve their full potential.

Lastly, this book and everything The Christophers do would not be possible without the support of our donors, and we thank you all for your tremendous generosity to us. As always, we keep you in our prayers.

Mary Ellen Robinson, Vice President
Father Dennis W. Cleary, M.M.

The Student and the Retiree

A car accident right before his freshman year of high school left Collin Smith permanently paralyzed from the chest down. Ernest Greene, a recent retiree who belonged to the same church as Smith's family, heard about the accident and felt "a calling" to help. Smith's overwhelmed parents welcomed the assistance, so Greene became Smith's caretaker and driver through his four years of high school.

As reported by *ABC News*, "When Smith entered North Carolina's High Point University, Greene started putting in 12-hour days, leaving his home before dawn to get to Smith's house by 6 a.m...He attended every class with Smith and took notes for him while pushing him three miles a day or more."

When Smith graduated from college in May 2013, Greene felt like a proud parent as he pushed his young charge across the stage. The school even gave Greene his own honorary diploma.

Regarding his special friend, Smith says, "Without him, I wouldn't have gotten where I needed to go...You just can't describe what we mean to each other."

A true friend sticks closer than one's nearest kin. (Proverbs 18:24)

Help me be a true friend to others, Jesus.

Getting Your Life Out of a Rut

Charles M. Schulz, creator of the *Peanuts* comic strip, put a lot of wisdom and laughs into his work.

For instance, in one strip, Charlie Brown visits Lucy's psychiatry booth and asks, "What can you do when you don't fit in? What can you do when life seems to be passing you by?"

"Follow me," Lucy tells Charlie Brown as she leads him to the top of a hill. "See the horizon over there? See how big this world is? See how much room there is for everybody? You were born to live in this world, right?"

"Right," responds Charlie Brown.

"WELL, LIVE IN IT THEN!" bellows Lucy. Then she adds, "Five cents, please."

If we feel like our lives are in a rut, it's easy to follow the Charlie Brown route and feel powerless and self-pitying. In this case, however, Lucy is the wise one.

Make the choice to change, then take action. All that's required is creativity and initiative. And maybe five cents.

My God, I seek You, my soul thirsts for You. (Psalm 63:1)

Give me the vision to see the right path for my life, Jesus.

The Archer with No Arms

Despite the fact that he was born without arms, Matt Stutzman wanted to learn archery after seeing his father and brother use bows for hunting. He did odd jobs around the family farm so he could save enough money to buy a bow for himself. Once he did, he figured out how to shoot it with his feet.

The 31-year-old Fairfield, Iowa, resident eventually got so good that he won a silver medal at the 2012 Paralympic Games in London. As reported by *NPR*, "Stutzman shoots from a seated position. He uses his left foot to put the arrow in place, then he pushes the compound bow away with his right foot and pulls the arrow back with a release aid that's strapped to his body."

Seeing Stutzman's archery skills is a sight to behold. And since he realizes that he can be an inspiration to others, that's just the way he wants it. He told *The Telegraph*, "Watching me, people can only say, 'I haven't got an excuse. I can't say my back's hurting or I got a sore finger; this guy's shooting arrows with no arms!' I hope I make everyone realize you can do whatever you want in this life if you just try."

**No one is crowned without competing.
(2 Timothy 2:5)**

Help me to be creative in surmounting obstacles, Jesus.

Who Sent the Bacon and Corn Meal?

In his book *The Sower's Seeds: 120 Inspiring Stories for Preaching, Teaching and Public Speaking,* Father Brian Cavanaugh shares this story from an unknown source:

"Years ago an old lady down south had no money to buy food. But with complete trust in God, she got down on her knees and prayed aloud, 'Dear Lord, please send me a side of bacon and a sack of corn meal.'

"One of the town's worst characters, overhearing her plea, decided to play a trick on her. Hurrying to the nearest store, he bought a side of bacon and a sack of corn meal. Upon his return to her home, he dropped the food down the chimney. It landed right in front of the hungry woman as she knelt in prayer.

"She exclaimed jubilantly: 'Oh Lord, you've answered my prayer!' Then she ran all around the neighborhood telling everyone the good news...The scoundrel ridiculed her before the whole town by telling how he had dropped the food down the chimney himself. The wise old woman quickly replied, 'Well, the devil may have brought it, but it was the Lord who sent it!'"

The Lord will provide. (Genesis 22:14)

Send us Your blessings, O Generous Creator.

A Bigger Purpose

Jeffrey Wright is a popular physics teacher at Louisville Male Traditional High School in Kentucky because he incorporates exploding pumpkins and other attention-grabbers into his lessons. Yet it's a simple lecture that makes the biggest impression on his students every year.

As reported in the *New York Times* and chronicled in the documentary *Wright's Law,* the teacher shares with his class the experience of being the father of a son, Adam, with a rare disorder that leaves him visually impaired and unable to speak or control his movements. Wright recalls his devastation at Adam's diagnosis. He wondered if there was even a purpose to life.

When Adam was four, Wright saw him playing with his sister and realized the boy had an inner life, after all. Wright and his wife taught him some sign language and, one day, Adam signed "I love you" to his father. That's when Wright learned life's purpose: love. He said, "When you look at physics, it's all about laws and how the world works. But [you have to]…tie those laws into a bigger purpose, the purpose in your heart."

Save me in Your steadfast love. (Psalm 31:16)

Lord, guide me in living out Your purpose for my life.

Making a Place in Heaven

Though Mary Sauter never had children of her own, the love she shows for the children of Albia, Iowa, conveys a motherly devotion. For more than 20 years, the retired teacher has been buying toys and clothes for the town's kids whose families can't afford them.

As reported by *NBC News's* Bob Dotson, Sauter spends $30,000 a year buying gifts: $10,000 of that total is from her savings, while the other $20,000 is from jobs such as tutoring. She's a bargain hunter who gets the most value from every dollar so she can help the maximum amount of people.

Perhaps that selflessness stems from her father, who adopted her from an Italian orphanage in 1957. Now 100 and practically blind, the father was welcomed into Sauter's home when he finally decided he couldn't live alone anymore.

For Sauter, the joy she sees on children's faces is reward enough for her efforts. Katie Della Vedova, one of her former students, says of her, "She's made her place in heaven."

May He defend the cause of the poor of the people, give deliverance to the needy. (Psalm 72:4)

Instill me with initiative and love, Father.

A Post-Christmas Prayer

The inspirational newsletter *Apple Seeds* featured this prayer—originally published in *Connections* magazine—for the days when the Christmas season comes to an end:

"Long after the angels disappear into the heavens, the shepherds return to their flocks, the Magi journey home and the great star sets, Jesus remains.

"The Child in whom we rediscover God's great love for humanity becomes the adult Redeemer who challenges us to imitate His selflessness and compassion in order that we might transform our world in love...

"May we allow the miracle of Christmas to continue long after the holiday trappings have been packed away. May we welcome the adult Messiah and His challenging Gospel to recreate our lives, making the peace, justice and hope of this holy season a reality in every season of the New Year. Amen."

Peace I leave with you; My peace I give to you. I do not give to you as the world gives. Do not let your hearts be troubled, and do not let them be afraid. (John 14:27)

Jesus, may I carry Your peace to others throughout the year.

A Good Word to Remember

"Why did this happen to this vibrant, intelligent, faith-filled man?" That's the question singer Amy Grant asked after her father, Dr. Burton Grant, was diagnosed with dementia.

A respected radiation oncologist, he had always loved singing, family togetherness, and prayers of gratitude. Writing in *Guideposts,* Amy said, "I never heard him say a negative word about another person. What a lesson that was." Now, Dr. Grant can't put two coherent sentences together.

"And yet," wrote Amy, "without words he is still teaching me one of the most important lessons of all: how to trust God in the smallest moments...even on those days when I don't understand a thing my father is saying except the word 'beautiful.'"

Amy then recalled standing arm-in-arm with her father on a sunny day on their farm, taking in their surroundings. "Beautiful," he said.

The truth of that moment struck his daughter's heart. Amy realized, "I guess if you're going to hang on to a short list of words, 'beautiful' is a good one."

Hope in the Lord. (Psalm 130:7)

Comfort and guide all caregivers and patients, Jesus.

Saved from a Kidnapper

When a five-year-old girl was kidnapped in Lancaster Township, Pennsylvania in July 2013, police officers and community members combed the streets looking for her. Temar Boggs, age 15, and his friend Chris Garcia decided to help too.

While searching the neighborhood on bicycles, Boggs noticed a car that was deliberately avoiding a police checkpoint. Boggs followed the car, getting close enough to see there was a little girl inside. When the driver noticed that Boggs and Garcia had spotted him, he pushed the girl out of the car and drove away. The girl ran to Boggs, who carried her to a police official and returned her to her grateful family.

Police caught the abductor who, it was discovered, had sexually assaulted the girl. If not for Boggs and Garcia, he might have done worse. The girl's family told *Lancaster Online* that Boggs is their hero. The humble teen responded, "I'm just a normal person who did a thing that anybody else would do...It was a blessing for me to make that happen."

Show yourself in all respects a model of good works. (Titus 2:7)

Instill us with the courage to pursue justice, Holy Spirit.

Do Me a Favor, Go to Uganda

Dr. Kevin Hunt, the brother of actress and talk show host Bonnie Hunt, practices Internal Medicine in Chicago. In 2005, he attended a Mass which was celebrated by Father Sam Okori, a Catholic priest from Northern Uganda who was in the United States taking pre-med classes.

When Dr. Hunt met Father Sam after Mass, he told the priest that he'd be happy to write him a letter of recommendation for medical school. Father Sam thanked him, then said, "Can you do me a favor? Can you go to Uganda with me? I'd like you to see my people and what health care is like there."

Dr. Hunt accepted Father Sam's offer. In conjunction with Uganda's Catholic Diocese of Lira, the two traveled there in 2007, and saw unsanitary conditions and a lack of basic medical supplies. As a result, Dr. Hunt and Father Sam created a foundation called Medical Aid to Northern Uganda (MANU) to raise funds. Dr. Hunt said, "Going somewhere that's foreign to help somebody else, you have to just take that leap of faith. It's one of the best things I ever did in my life."

He sought the good of his nation.
(1 Maccabees 14:4)

Savior, open my heart to the suffering of others.

Jennifer Lawrence's Biggest Fan

Academy Award-winning actress Jennifer Lawrence grew up in Louisville, Kentucky, and hasn't let success distract her from the friends she made there. In fact, she still stays in close touch with Andy Strunk, a young man with Down Syndrome whom she got to know in church.

Strunk's mother, Pollyanna, told New York's *Daily News,* "[Jennifer] always had a soft heart for him. She looked out for him. Middle school is a tough place to be, especially for a kid with special needs." Lawrence even got Strunk crowned the school's king for a day by nominating him and campaigning for him.

Since Lawrence's Hollywood success, Strunk has become a local celebrity in his own right. While being profiled by local TV station *WAVE3,* he called Lawrence with the cameras rolling. She sounded thrilled to hear from him and told the reporter, "He has the kindest heart of anybody I've ever met, he's always in a good mood, and he's one of the funniest people I've ever been around."

If you know someone with special needs, follow Jennifer Lawrence's example and be a loving, supportive friend to them.

Love kindness. (Micah 6:8)

Teach me what it means to be a true friend, Lord.

The Value of Compliments

Writing on the *Verily* magazine blog, Ashley Crouch reflected on a recent report from the Harvard Medical Association, which found that "gratitude helps us refocus on what we have instead of what we lack. Those who count their blessings have less likelihood for depression, anxiety, or envy, while possessing stronger social connections, greater relationship satisfaction, and a real leg up in the workplace."

Crouch then cited psychologist Dr. John Gottman who, after researching thousands of couples, discovered that those who complimented each other the most "reported the highest satisfaction...Conflict will happen in any relationship, but major research on emotional psychology discovered that it can be easier to offer criticism when both parties rest secure in their affection towards one another." Dr. Gottman noted that couples who rarely compliment each other often wind up with serious marital problems that can even lead to divorce.

The lesson? If you want successful relationships, remember to build each other up, not tear each other down.

A cheerful heart is a good medicine.
(Proverbs 17:22)

Holy Spirit, open my eyes to the good in everyone.

A Swab to Save a Life

Losing a young cousin to cancer motivated Austin Luera to take part in Senior Swab Day at Loyola Blakefield High School in Towson, Maryland. The bone marrow drive collected DNA samples by swabbing students' cheeks. They were then entered into a database to be possible bone marrow donors in the future.

During his freshman year at the University of South Carolina, Luera learned his bone marrow was a match for an eight-year-old boy fighting leukemia. Despite the pain and recovery time involved in donating bone marrow, he decided to do whatever he could to save this child's life.

Luera told *The Catholic Review*, "They made two incisions on either side of my hip bone and went in 15 times on each side to extract the necessary bone marrow...I might feel a little pain for a few weeks, but when you have a young person dealing with something much more serious, you need to think beyond yourself and do what you can to help them."

Render service with enthusiasm, as to the Lord. (Ephesians 6:7)

Father, give me the courage to endure pain to benefit someone in need.

Tornado Can't Destroy Hope

Hearing the story of Nancy Davis taught *National Review* writer Kathryn Jean Lopez a lesson about hope. Davis, age 94, lost her home in the tornado that hit Moore, Oklahoma, on May 20, 2013. Unfortunately, this wasn't the first time that happened. Her house had also been destroyed during a tornado in 1999.

As the 2013 storm approached, Davis invited several neighbors, including a pregnant woman and two-year-old boy, into her storm shelter where they all rode out the 210-mile-per-hour winds. When the tornado was over, she discovered a stack of $100 bills. Instead of keeping them all for herself, she handed them out to others who had lost their homes as well.

What did all this teach Lopez? She writes, "Part of the reason we rush to watch scenes of devastation on live television is that we need to know how people begin again...What is it that gives people reason to rejoice when they have lost what seems like everything? Hope. Gratitude. Faith in a destination so much greater than what we can see around us, so much more beautiful than the most radiant gem you can conjure up."

My hope is in You. (Psalm 39:7)

When all seems lost, Jesus, be my hope.

Not a Friend, But a Father

When Patheos.com blogger Calah Alexander was going through a rebellious teen period that led her to constantly challenge her parents' rules, she once declared to her father, "I hate you." Though she could tell he was hurt, he simply responded, "If your hate is the price I have to pay to get you to do the right thing, I'll pay it. Even if you hate me forever, I will never stop pushing you to be good."

Many years later, Alexander—now a parent herself—reflected on what that incident taught her about the love of both her earthly and heavenly fathers.

She wrote, "Those words were the most powerful ones my father ever said to me...He loved me so much that he wanted what was best for me, not what would make me happy, not what would make me love him more. He loved me unselfishly...not because I was such a joy to be around. Not because I was obedient, or even tolerable at that age. He loved me because I was his daughter, and nothing I could do would ever change that."

For the Lord reproves the one He loves. (Proverbs 3:12)

Instill parents with wisdom and selflessness, Father.

The Overlooked Cleaning Woman

The inspirational newsletter *Apple Seeds* shared a story about a smart and conscientious college student whose professor gave a surprise quiz one day. The student answered all the questions with ease until she came to the last one: "What is the name of the woman who cleans this floor of the building?"

The student was familiar with the cleaning woman, whom she'd seen many times. She even remembered what she looked like: tall, dark hair, in her 50s. But she didn't know her name so she left the answer blank.

Following the quiz, another student complained about the last question, hoping it wouldn't count towards her grade. The professor responded that it absolutely would count toward her grade, adding, "In your careers you will meet many people. All of them are significant! They deserve your attention and care, even if all you can do is smile and say hello!"

The student never forgot that lesson. She also never forgot that the cleaning woman's name was Dorothy.

**Love your neighbor as yourself.
(Galatians 5:14)**

Remind me that all people are created in Your image and likeness, Father, and therefore deserve my respect.

Unmasking the Idols in Your Life

In her book *Strange Gods: Unmasking the Idols in Everyday Life,* author Elizabeth Scalia explores our tendency to make gods of ideology, money, technology, sex, pride and more. One of the ways she combats her personal idols is by invoking the presence of God whenever possible.

Scalia learned that practice when she and her husband arranged for a police officer to talk with a teen group at their church. The officer said that every time he gets called to a domestic disturbance, he asks Jesus to stand between the couple who are fighting. The reason: "Jesus is peace, and He will bring His peace into this situation in one way or another."

Scalia said on *Christopher Closeup,* "The officer said this has never failed and he uses this in his life now. I do too...Even when I'm in a grocery store and I see something like a kid yelling at the mother, I'll think, 'Jesus, stand between them.'"

Scalia hopes her book makes readers ask, "Is something standing between me and God? If so, isn't it something that I should move to the side so I can look at Jesus and have that relationship with Him that He is calling me toward?"

Return to Me...rend your hearts. (Joel 2:12,13)

Keep my vision and heart focused on You, Jesus.

How Boots Are Like Marriage

When Kathy Tuan-Maclean's soon-to-be fiancé gave her L.L. Bean boots for Christmas many years ago, she wasn't initially impressed. Even though they felt warm, they were clunky and unfashionable. Still, she wore them for the next two decades of marriage through snow and ice.

Then, in the winter of 2010, Tuan-Maclean decided she wanted cute boots. They made her very happy—until they sprang a leak during their third winter.

Disappointed in her relatively new purchase, she complained to her husband, who confirmed the value of the L.L. Bean boots. "That's why I got them for you—they're practical and sturdy and will last forever, just like me," he said.

Tuan-Maclean realized that her marriage, like those boots, isn't flashy; it's built for endurance, for hardship, and for the long haul.

When you choose the person you want to marry, look beyond the surface and go for the one that's built to last.

Love...bears all things, believes all things, hopes all things, endures all things.
(1 Corinthians 13:7)

Jesus, guide us to spouses who will love us like You do.

Walking Through Hell with a Smile

Amanda Berry, Gina DeJesus and Michelle Knight were kidnapped, held captive, raped and violently abused by a Cleveland, Ohio man for 10 years. Upon their escape in May 2013, they requested privacy so they could focus on reconnecting with their families and rebuilding their lives. The Cleveland Courage Fund was established to help each of them financially.

In July 2013, the young women got together to record a video thanking all those who had helped them, saying they appreciated the public's "love and kindness."

Michelle Knight said, "I may have been through hell and back, but I am strong enough to walk through hell with a smile on my face and my head held high...I don't want to be consumed by hatred. With that being said, we need to take a leap of faith and know that God is in control. We have been hurt by people, but we need to rely on God as being the judge. God has a plan for all of us. The plan that He gave me was to help others that have been in the same situation. I am in control of my own destiny with the guidance of God."

You will be able to endure. (Exodus 18:23)

Heal our wounds, Savior, and help us trust in You.

God Told Me What to Say

When Sister Mary Antona Ebo was about to celebrate her 89th birthday last year, she was off for a few days to Washington, D.C., where she talked about the time she marched with Dr. Martin Luther King. She spends quite a few days talking about that experience, in fact, because she regards it as a centerpiece in her life.

"I think that's why I've lived this long, because I've got a story to tell you," she said to her Washington audience. And it is quite a story at that. Sister Mary Antona, from St. Louis, recalled being in Selma, Alabama, responding to Dr. King's call for a peaceful protest to answer the then-recent Bloody Sunday violence. And how, as the only black nun in her group, she became a de facto spokesman when TV reporters peppered her with questions.

"All I know was that I was scared to death," she remembers. "But God told me what to say, and it went around the world."

She'll keep on saying what God wants her to as long as she's able to do it. As she notes: "Beware of being silent."

For it is God who is at work in you. (Philippians 2:13)

Abba, grant us the courage to speak out against injustice.

That's Not What I Wanted

If you're frustrated that you didn't make the positive life changes you wanted, blame your mind.

The late Dr. Edmund Bergler, psychologist and author, described the phenomenon as "the human tendency to find a strange, deeply unconscious satisfaction in displeasure." In other words, our mind tricks us out of what we want—and often to our own detriment.

In some cases, we tell ourselves we can't do something or don't deserve to do it. At other times, we convince ourselves that happiness can't last, so why bother to change, or that certain actions are selfish, and we feel guilty. Sometimes our mind even justifies our wrong actions, or the hurtful actions of others toward us.

How can we "trick" our minds back to right thinking? Be aware of the negative—and think positive instead. Certainly our loving God wants nothing but the best for each one of us.

Now set your mind and heart to seek the Lord your God. (1 Chronicles 22:19)

Open my heart to Your love, Lord.

Good Counsel Homes

In 1979, Chris Bell was working in a Times Square shelter with homeless and runaway kids when a young mother with a baby approached him asking for help.

The young woman explained that when she found out she was pregnant, she was happy because she thought that she and her boyfriend would start a life together. Instead, her boyfriend's response to the pregnancy was, "Get rid of this thing."

Alone and depressed, the young woman considered killing herself, then realized she couldn't do that to the innocent baby inside her. Thrown out of the house by her own mother soon after the baby was born, she had nowhere to turn.

Bell told her he would help, but soon discovered there was very little assistance available for mothers and babies in similar situations. That's what led him to start Good Counsel Homes, which offer shelter, care and career counseling to homeless, expectant and new mothers with children in New York and New Jersey. They continue to offer help or guidance to anyone who calls their toll free number at 1-800-723-8331.

**Let the little children come to Me.
(Matthew 19:14)**

Help me to be a lifeline to those in need, Jesus.

Angel on the Road

The year was 1977. A tremendous blizzard blanketed the Northeastern United States, leaving three feet of snow, icy roads and downed power lines in its wake. The city of Buffalo, New York, was hit particularly hard.

Dennis J. Morrison's future mother-in-law, Ruth, was at her friend's playing bridge. Long used to Buffalo's treacherous weather, Ruth ventured out to take the short drive home. When she found the way to her street blocked, she decided to walk. Then a stranger appeared, warning her that the path to her home was too dangerous to walk alone. He guided Ruth around fallen trees and power lines, and got her safely to her front door. No one knew this man, and he was never seen again.

In *The Catholic Times*, Morrison wrote that Ruth said of this stranger, "He was my Guardian Angel, whose job that evening was to see to it that I arrived home safely."

Thirty-five years later, at age 96, Ruth passed away. While her family grieved, they were all assured her Guardian Angel was waiting to take her "home" once again.

I am going to send an angel in front of you, to guard you. (Exodus 23:20)

Jesus, may we always give thanks for our guardian angels.

Happiness Changes with Age

Heidi Grant Halvorson, age 40, has a confession to make: spending Saturday nights at home watching old movies or playing with her seven-year-old makes her happy. She realizes that her 20-year-old self would be horrified by how boring that sounds, but in fact, studies show it's completely normal.

Writing in *The Atlantic,* Halvorson notes that three psychologists analyzed expressions of happiness over 12 million personal blogs: "Younger bloggers described experiences of happiness as being times when they felt excited, ecstatic, or elated—the way you feel when you're anticipating the joys the future will bring...Older bloggers were more inclined to describe happy moments of feeling peaceful, relaxed, calm, or relieved. This kind of happiness is less about what lies ahead, and more about being content in your current circumstances."

Halvorson concludes, "If you're like me, and you find that your life has become more about pursuing peace and relaxation than giddy excitement, rest assured that you aren't missing out on happiness. Your happiness has evolved, just as you have."

**Happy are those who find wisdom.
(Psalm 3:13)**

Lord, help me appreciate life's simple pleasures.

Sit Less, Live Longer

If you're sitting down while reading this, you might want to stand up when you're done. In fact, if you sit a lot in general—at work, for instance—you need to consider adding a new routine to your day.

As reported in *Spry* magazine, studies have shown that "people who spend extended periods on their duffs are about twice as likely to develop type two diabetes, heart disease and early death—even if they exercise regularly."

That may sound frightening, but some relatively simple solutions can remedy the problem: "Breaking up your day with two-minute periods of activity will do the trick. Set a timer to go off every 30-60 minutes to prompt you to stretch your legs. Every four hours, take a 10-minute stroll. And make a habit of standing during TV commercials, phone calls—even business meetings if your co-workers are game."

God created us body and soul. Be sure to care for both.

If there is a physical body, there is also a spiritual body. (1 Corinthians 15:44)

Guide me in creating new routines that benefit my body, mind and spirit, Creator.

God Leads Us By Strange Ways

Cardinal John Henry Newman once offered the following insight about finding our unique path to happiness by trusting in God:

"God knows what is my greatest happiness, but I do not. There is no rule about what is happy and good; what suits one would not suit another. And the ways by which perfection is reached vary very much; the medicines necessary for our souls are very different from each other.

"Thus God leads us by strange ways; we know He wills our happiness, but we neither know what our happiness is, nor the way. We are blind; left to ourselves we should take the wrong way; we must leave it to Him."

Sometimes the unexpected paths we follow in life lead us to the greatest happiness. Put your trust in our Heavenly Father, and let Him show you the way.

Those who know Your name put their trust in You, for You, O Lord, have not forsaken those who seek You. (Matthew 7:7)

I like being in control, Lord. Instill me with the humility to surrender to Your will.

The Miracle Baby

A womb infection caused Carolyn Isbister of Great Britain to go into premature labor at 24 weeks gestation. Her daughter Rachael was born weighing only 20 ounces.

As reported by the London-based *Daily Mail,* the baby's heart "was beating once every 10 seconds and she was not breathing." Doctors informed Isbister that Rachael would likely die within 20 minutes. The grief-stricken mother noticed that her daughter felt cold, so she laid the baby on her chest to warm her up. Then, the seemingly impossible happened.

The warmth of Carolyn's body caused Rachael's heart to start beating correctly and enabled her to breathe on her own. Carolyn recalled, "The doctors came in and said there was still no hope, but I wasn't letting go of her. We had her blessed by the hospital chaplain, and waited for her to slip away."

Rachael had other plans, though. After a four-month stay in the hospital, she grew to normal baby weight and went home. One doctor said, "I have seen nothing like this in my 27 years of practice. That mother's love saved her baby."

Love...hopes all things. (1 Corinthians 13:7)

Allow us to feel the healing embrace of Your love, Lord.

Seniors Find Satisfaction in Volunteering

All across the nation, more and more programs geared towards assisting the elderly are comprised of volunteers who are senior citizens themselves. *Catholic News Service* journalist Liz O'Connor gives a few examples of some of these participants.

"Sue Jepson, 70, is legally blind and has some difficulty walking," O'Connor notes, "but that doesn't stop her from being active in several organizations and volunteering three or four days a week."

"I just like helping others," Jepson explains in an interview from her Catholic Charities-affiliated home in Portland, Oregon.

Cindy Hamberg, 64, who heads an osteoporosis prevention organization at the Winona, Minnesota branch of Catholic Charities, also attests to the benefits of seniors volunteering.

"I love it, I really love it," she exclaims. "What a powerful feeling volunteering is!"

No matter your age, find meaning and purpose in your life by assisting others.

Let them...work honestly with their own hands, so as to have something to share with the needy. (Ephesians 4:28)

Jesus, guide us to respect and comfort the elderly.

The Last Word

Some 20 years ago, Joyce Holman decided to take stock. Her life was a mess. She'd been in and out of jails for most of it, all for nonviolent offenses related to her drug habit. Mother of two grown children, she asked herself how a grandmother could wind up in jail. She resolved to turn things around.

For openers, she swore off drugs—and has been sober for 20 years. She got a GED, a degree and a steady, well-paying job. She started a program to help former addicts like herself. And Holman, a New Jerseyan, resolved to ask Gov. Chris Christie for a pardon.

Her hard work and good example paid off handsomely. The governor, impressed, granted the pardon and hailed her as "a beacon" for the state.

Holman's response was simple. "I never thought that I would be deserving of this but God always comes through," she said. "He always has the last word."

I have come not to call the righteous but sinners to repentance. (Luke 5:32)

Father, may we never doubt Your infinite capacity to forgive.

Giving God Room to Work

When *American Idol* producers told Season 11 contestants that making religious comments on social media could hurt them with viewers, Colton Dixon ignored the warning. "That's the only reason I was there," he said during an interview on *Christopher Closeup*. "It was amazing to see God work and use us as tools on a TV show in front of 20 million people."

Dixon earned seventh place on *Idol* that season, and is now establishing himself in the Christian music industry by writing and singing songs grounded in the challenges he's experienced: "We've all gone through something that has broken us down, but I love realizing that I'm broken because that gives room for God to work and fill you up with His love."

Though Dixon wants to be a witness for Christ, he admits he falls short sometimes so people should be wary of putting too much faith in him. He said, "What outsiders looking in on us have to realize is that you're not following us; you're following Jesus. We're not perfect and we're never going to be. We're trying just like everyone else."

The Lord is near to the brokenhearted. (Psalm 34:18)

Redeemer, use my brokenness to fill me with Your love.

"The Blind Side's" Super Ending

Many people have seen the Christopher Award-winning movie *The Blind Side,* which told the story of Sean and Leigh Anne Tuohy (played by Tim McGraw and Sandra Bullock) adopting homeless African-American teen Michael Oher, supporting him and his education, and helping to launch his football career with the Baltimore Ravens.

The Tuohys met resistance because they were white and Oher was black, but they ignored the criticism and created a happy ending by both Hollywood and real-life standards. That ending got happier on Feb. 3, 2013, when the Ravens won the Super Bowl with help from Oher, whose adopted family was with him.

After the game, Leigh Anne Tuohy told *ABC News* that she, her husband and their biological children were overjoyed at Michael's success. Tuohy said, "You don't have to look like someone else to love them...There are wonderful kids all over this country and this world that want a forever family. We believe there are no unwanted kids; there are just unfound families."

Whoever welcomes one such child in My name welcomes Me. (Matthew 18:5)

Help us to see beyond superficial differences, Father.

A Navy Veteran's Tough Times

James Blakely, a long-ago Navy veteran who had lived through the Pearl Harbor attack, had come on tough times. In civilian life he had married, raised a family, and been ordained a Baptist minister. But now, in his nineties, he'd been fleeced out of his home and was living in New York in a rusty trailer with no running water.

One more thing: he was a black man, and he remembered what the old segregated Navy was like. He and fellow blacks were relegated to mess hall and related duties. It didn't concern him, though: "I was too busy worrying about the Japanese."

Then Denis Hamill wrote about him in New York's *Daily News,* and suddenly life took a turn for the better. Among other things, Blakely got a new home courtesy of the city, complete with shower, a stove, and air-conditioning. Hamill's column, tracing the lifeline of a Navy veteran of Pearl Harbor, had done the trick. "I have keys," Blakely said. "Boy, oh boy. It's a long time since I had keys to a place of my own."

No matter how bleak your prospects, trust in the Lord.

Rejoice in hope. (Romans 12:12)

Messiah, may we remember that every troubled soul has a story.

A Groundhog Day Awakening

Though he had a family and a career he loved, Paul Hannam felt restless and unfulfilled—yet he didn't know why. One night, he and his wife watched the movie *Groundhog Day*, which stars Bill Murray as an arrogant weatherman mysteriously forced to repeatedly relive the same day; it leaves him even more miserable than he already is. Finally, Murray wakes up and realizes that if he's stuck reliving Groundhog Day anyway, he might as well make it the best day possible. In other words, he chooses gratitude instead of misery. That makes all the difference, and allows him to move forward with his life.

Writing in *Guideposts*, Hannam says, "I thought back to all [my] successes...Had I ever given thanks for them? And what about my family?...There was no earthly reason for my misery."

Hannam concludes, "I've come to appreciate all that I've been given and all that I can give to others. It goes back to what I learned from *Groundhog Day*, that choice I make every morning. Let me make today the best day possible. And you know what? It is."

Give thanks to the Lord. (1 Chronicles 16:34)

Help me be grateful for my blessings, Holy Spirit.

No Greater Love or Glory

On January 23rd, 1943, a U.S. Army troop ship sailed off the coast of New York, bound for Greenland. Four chaplains were also on board that fateful night: Father John P. Washington, a Catholic priest; Rabbi Alexander D. Goode; Rev. Clark V. Poling, a minister of the Reformed Church; and Rev. George L. Fox of the Methodist Church. Armed with faith in God, these men proved to be true heroes a few short weeks later.

When a German submarine torpedoed their ship on February 3rd, the four chaplains rushed on deck to assist, even going so far as to give up their life jackets. These men of God were last seen holding hands on deck and praying. In 1944, they were posthumously awarded the Purple Heart and Distinguished Service Cross.

"Certainly the chaplains did something huge," Father Joseph Mancini, pastor of St. Stephen's Church in Kearny, New Jersey, told *Catholic New York* reporter Claudia McDonnell. "We don't have to do something that huge, but in the small things, we're all capable of that same ideal."

I have fought the good fight...kept the faith. (2 Timothy 4:7)

Lord, bless and safeguard our nation's military chaplains.

Prayer Before Starting Work

Today we'd like to share a prayer for the beginning of your work day. The writer is unknown:

"My Heavenly Father, as I enter this workplace I bring Your presence with me. I speak Your peace, Your grace, Your mercy, and Your perfect order into this office. I acknowledge Your power over all that will be spoken, thought, decided and done within these walls.

"Lord, I thank You for the gifts You have blessed me with. I commit to using them responsibly in Your honor. Give me a fresh supply of strength to do my job. Anoint my projects, ideas and energy so that even my smallest accomplishment may bring You glory.

"Lord, when I am confused, guide me. When I am weary, energize me. When I am burned out, infuse me with the light of the Holy Spirit. May the work that I do and the way I do it bring faith, joy and a smile to all that I come in contact with today. Amen."

Now begin the work, and the Lord be with you. (1 Chronicles 22:16)

Help me find joy in my labor, Lord.

How This Teen Might Save Your Life

Having lost both an uncle and a family friend to pancreatic cancer, 15-year-old Jack Andraka from Crownsville, Maryland, knew that the disease was often fatal because of a lack of early detection. While sitting in his North County High School biology class one day, the scientifically-inclined teen came upon the idea to develop a test involving antibodies and "carbon nanotubes."

Following extensive research, he sent a letter explaining his theory to 200 professors at Johns Hopkins University and the National Institutes of Health, asking for lab assistance. All the professors but one rejected him. With support from Dr. Anirban Maitra, Andraka devised a specially designed paper sensor that checks blood and urine for a biomarker that indicates pancreatic cancer. The test takes five minutes to run, costs three cents, and is 400 times more sensitive than current tests.

If pancreatic cancer patients in the future get life-saving treatment, they can be grateful for Jack Andraka's intelligence, initiative and refusal to take no for an answer.

**Give me now wisdom and knowledge.
(2 Chronicles 1:10)**

Bring comfort and healing to all cancer patients, Lord.

The Angry Driver's Surprise

On Facebook, a man named Garry shared the following story about his encounter with an impatient driver:

"I bought a very irritated women a latte this morning. I was on my way to a client meeting in Farmington Hills, and as I made a lane change, she sped up to keep me out of the lane. We were coming up to a red light, and my nose was already in the lane when she tried to cut me off, but she had a good time honking at me."

"I pulled into the Starbucks drive-thru for a double tall mocha...and she pulled in right behind me. When I came to the window I paid for her drink as well as mine, and then for several miles down the highway, I was still smiling. It was a better choice than road rage :-)"

It isn't easy to answer rudeness with kindness, but it can be the best, most peaceful option. It may also leave you smiling.

Wisdom will come into your heart, and knowledge will be pleasant to your soul; prudence will watch over you; and understanding will guard you. (Proverbs 2:10-11)

Help me to control my temper, Father, so that I may be a loving example to others.

Date the Unexpected One

When seeking a relationship, it's only natural to imagine the perfect *looking* person over the perfect person for you. But what about your compatibility in areas like finances and lifestyle? Do you both see child-rearing in your future, or spending time together in excitement and boredom?

Writer J.R. Baldwin suggests that if you want true love and romance, you have to prepare for it. How?

- Close your eyes, and don't just judge by looks. Are you interested in this person because of their availability and their ambitions? Their sense of humor and their smile?

- Don't worry whether he or she is "the one." First, genuinely enjoy getting to know the other person and pray about the relationship. Keep an open mind to a future, and discuss things that matter.

- Pray for God to guide your mind and heart.

Remember, the first step toward love comes from being open to a person as God sees them, not as you want to see them.

Seek Me with all your heart. (Jeremiah 29:13)

Lord, protect my heart and give me the courage to seek and give love.

A Good Samaritan Doctor

One of the people *NBC News* correspondent Bob Dotson highlights in his book *American Story* is Jack McConnell, a doctor who retired to Hilton Head Island, South Carolina.

While talking to one of the island's 6,000 working poor, Dr. McConnell discovered that most of them couldn't afford medical care, so they would go to the emergency room when they were sick. The physician knew that was fine if you broke a leg, but inefficient if you needed a check-up or preventive care.

Dr. McConnell asked his fellow retired doctors, "Why don't we open up a clinic and volunteer?" Their initial response was that they had gotten out from under burdensome insurance costs and didn't want to open themselves up to lawsuits.

Dr. McConnell appealed to South Carolina's legislature to let him operate a clinic under the state's Good Samaritan law, which states that you can't sue a doctor who stops to help you in an emergency situation. The law passed and the clinic opened. Today, 44 states have similar free clinics because of Dr. Jack McConnell's efforts.

Honor physicians for their services. (Sirach 38:1)

Bless caring physicians, Divine Healer.

A Stable Life at the Ranch

Though they have two biological children, Julie and Rusty Bulloch have also welcomed nearly 30 teens and young adults into their Lakeland, Florida home and ranch over the past 16 years. Why? To provide them with a stable family life — or to help them get away from gang life or drugs.

The Bullochs didn't adopt or foster these young people, but rather worked in conjunction with their mothers, who knew their kids needed help. During an interview on *Christopher Closeup* about their reality television show *Bulloch Family Ranch*, Julie explained, "We always uplift the mom."

Fathers, on the other hand, are part of the problem, especially since an estimated 95 percent of the Bullochs' "kids" come from broken homes. Rusty said, "We've actually had some of the kids say, 'If we didn't steal, we didn't eat.' When you look at it like that, how can you blame that kid for surviving? I blame the dad for not being there and bringing them up in a godly home and leading them in the right way."

Be a positive influence in the lives of young people.

Fathers make known to children your faithfulness. (Isaiah 38:19)

Help fathers be responsible parents, Lord.

Only Chocolate Should Be Bitter

If Valentine's Day finds you single and resentful of the people who will be making gooey eyes at each other on February 14, *Verily* magazine's Monica Gabriel has some advice. As a young, single woman herself, she notes, "Bitterness only makes a person happy when it comes in the form of baking chocolate."

Here are some of Gabriel's survival tips:

- "Don't make it all about you. Instead of wallowing, I will send a card or flowers to a single girlfriend or sister. Just because it's not from 'The One,' does not mean I won't make them feel loved."

- "Plan a night out with friends. Valentine's Day is a wonderful excuse to gather all available friends—boys and girls—to celebrate being single and being loved."

- "Be kind to yourself. I don't have to pretend that being single for the rest of my life would make me perfectly happy. But [not having someone to share] a candlelight dinner with this Valentine's Day does not mean that I am unlovable. I feel hopeful and loved every other day of the year, why should Valentine's Day be any different?"

Do not let your hearts be troubled. (John 14:1)

Bring companionship to the lonely, Lord.

Avoiding the Worry Generator

Odd Thomas is one of best-selling author Dean Koontz's most beloved characters because he retains his hope, humor and faith despite witnessing some horrific crimes.

In the book, *Odd Apocalypse*, Odd Thomas shares his thoughts about trusting God. The advice can apply to anyone tempted by negative thinking.

Koontz writes, "Without faith to act as a governor, the human mind is a runaway worry generator, a dynamo of negative expectations...If you entertain too much anxiety about too many things, if you place no trust in providence, what you fear will more often come to pass. We make so many of our own troubles, from mere mishaps to disasters, by dwelling on the possibility of them until the possible becomes the inevitable. Therefore I told myself to stop worrying...to place myself in the care of providence...If we are in a condition of complete simplicity (as the poet T.S. Eliot said), hope and trust will more reliably keep a man afloat, while fear is more likely to sink him."

Cast all your anxiety on Him. (1 Peter 5:7)

Increase my trust in You, Compassionate Redeemer.

A Personal Gift for Valentine's Day

With Valentine's Day approaching, you may want to consider writing a love letter to your spouse. That's the suggestion of Patheos.com blogger Pat Gohn, who relishes the letters she received from her husband years ago.

The reason, Gohn writes, is "because all couples long for communion with one another, especially the kind that will last. That simply cannot happen without communication that starts off with words that come from the heart."

Though Gohn offers tips for men to write love letters to women, her insights can also be applied the other way around:

- "What is the one memory of your loved one that stays with you and lifts you up when you think of him/her?"

- "How does his/her love make you a better person?"

- "How does his/her care make you feel loved by him/her? By God?"

- "What is his/her greatest virtue?"

Regardless of the time of year, offer your loved ones words and actions from the heart.

**Love one another deeply from the heart.
(1 Peter 1:22)**

Holy Spirit, fill me with loving words.

Saving a Suicidal Man

Kevin Berthia felt such despair that he was ready to end it all. In March 2005, he climbed over the railing of the Golden Gate Bridge so he could jump to his death into San Francisco Bay.

Before making that final decision, however, Berthia heard the voice of California Highway Patrol Officer Kevin Briggs. The cop, who had talked hundreds of people out of committing suicide over the years, knew that Berthia needed someone to listen, really listen to him. They started an hour-long discussion, which resulted in Berthia choosing life.

In May 2013, Briggs and Berthia were reunited at the American Foundation for Suicide Prevention public service ceremony. It was the first time they'd seen each other since that fateful day. Briggs was delighted to learn that Berthia was now happily married with two children.

He had taken a path to mental healing that never would have happened without the compassionate police officer, who years ago had told him, "You have to seek some help. [And then] you're getting better. And you can have a life."

Your help has made me great. (Psalm 18:35)

Send lifelines to those feeling despair, Savior.

Where Forgiveness and Love Rule

Reflecting on her 12th wedding anniversary with her husband, Dan, blogger Hallie Lord offered these insights:

"In a sense, life has matured us to a far greater degree over the past decade than I ever could have imagined. Life poured six babies into our hearts; Life asked us to trust him (and each other) as we wrestled with a decade of financial hardship; Life asked us to travel from state to state as we sought the place in which the earth would invite us to put down roots; and Life said, 'I know this is hard, love each other anyway.' And we did."

"Imperfectly, of course. I cringe when I think of the things I've said and the damage I've caused, but my sweet husband has remained emphatic that forgiveness and love rule our home. He has taught me how to leave the pain behind and march forward with him, hand in hand. There are moments in life when God lifts you up and gives you a moment of ecstatic clarity. These are the moments that give all those crosses meaning and reveal their goodness."

Have unity of spirit, sympathy, love for one another, a tender heart and a humble mind. (1 Peter 3:8)

Help my spouse and I grow in love for each other, Savior.

How to Get Good at Something

Though Jerry Seinfeld rose to fame as the star of his own TV show, he worked for years as a stand-up comedian learning his craft. During an interview with *Entertainment Weekly,* he recalled his early days hoping that some veteran comedian could offer him guidance. In retrospect, he realizes there was no adequate advice that would have made telling jokes in front of an audience any easier.

Seinfeld said, "There's no training, there were no classes, there was no getting ready—it was sink or swim. You had to learn how to do it well to survive. And that, in my opinion, is the only healthy path to becoming a comedian. If you grow up in a family where you have lots of privileges and there's money around...you're never going to get good at anything."

Seinfeld's insight can be applied to anyone, not just comedians. If we want to excel at something, it will only happen through determined and persistent practice. Having everything come easy is actually a deterrent to quality. Trial, error, failure and struggle will make you a master of your craft.

Let us run with perseverance. (Hebrews 12:1)

Help me endure failure on the road to success, Father.

Medal Quest

Since 1948, the Paralympics have brought together the world's top athletes with physical disabilities in thrilling, high-level competitions. Today, the games are held every two years in coordination with the Olympics and at Olympic stadiums. Yet, the Paralympics are often called "the Olympics no one knows."

PBS/WGBH's online project *Medal Quest* aimed to change that oversight by highlighting the American athletes who trained for and competed in London's 2012 Paralympic Games. Executive Producer Judith Vecchione explained, "One of our goals...was to encourage audiences to reconsider their ideas about ability and disability. As they witnessed the [competitors'] intense training, commitment and skill...viewers also learned about athletes giving back to their communities and becoming role models."

The Christophers honored *Medal Quest* with our 2013 Christopher Spirit Award for highlighting the heart, spirit and potential inside a group of athletes whose abilities are far greater than their disabilities.

Run with perseverance the race that is set before us. (Hebrews 12:1-2)

Lord, turn my challenges into stepping stones to greatness.

A Modern Form of Slavery

Though thousands of football fans came to New Orleans prior to the 2013 Super Bowl between the Ravens and 49ers, government, church and civic groups were also there for a different reason: to combat the victimization of girls and women forced into prostitution.

As reported by *America* magazine, experts estimated that 10,000 prostitutes descended on Miami when the Super Bowl was held there in 2010. Many were sex trafficking victims.

John Krentel, a New Orleans attorney who serves on the board for Eden House, which helps women escaping prostitution, said, "Human trafficking is basically a form of slavery...I want to emphasize, these are American citizens we are talking about."

Laura J. Lederer, president of the advocacy group Global Centurion Foundation, adds, "We need to reach young men and boys...and help them understand that human beings should never be bought and sold. We're trying to reach people from a values-based, faith-based and human rights-based approach about the sacredness, worth and dignity of every human being."

Rescue the oppressed. (Isaiah 1:17)

Savior, lead victims of slavery to freedom.

A Poem as Lovely as a Tree

There was a time when every student could have recited the opening lines of "Trees"—"I think that I shall never see/A poem lovely as a tree..."

Time was, too, when schoolchildren could have told you that the poem was written by Joyce Kilmer, a New Jerseyan and convert to the Catholic faith, killed in action in World War I.

"Trees" and Kilmer were back in the news last year on the 100th anniversary of the poem—February 2, 2013—when Mahwah, New Jersey, declared that the poem was written in the township. Mahwah has plenty of proof for its claim. Not only did Kilmer reside there; he was in his Mahwah home the day the poem was written. But while Mahwah has this evidence on its side, it also has an equal amount of contradictory opinions. Several towns claim the honor of inspiring the poem, as do at least two well-known universities: Rutgers and Notre Dame.

Whatever its origin, "Trees" endures to inspire new generations. As its closing lines declare: "Poems are made by fools like me/But only God can make a tree."

Long ago You laid the foundation of the earth, and the heavens are the work of Your hands. (Psalm 102:25)

Glory to Your everlasting works, Creator.

Father Dollar Bill

They used to call him Father Dollar Bill. That wasn't his real name, of course, which was Father Maurice Chase. Once a proficient fund-raiser in the Los Angeles Archdiocese, he earned his unusual nickname by giving out—you guessed it—dollar bills. He was in his nineties when he died a few years ago, and he brushed aside critics who said his charity might be laudable but that it had no "long-term impact."

"I'm just trying to give them hope," Father Dollar Bill would reply. "To give them a sense of dignity."

The "them" he referred to were his Skid Row recipients, and how they missed him when he was gone. "He was just a glorious man," said one woman. "He was always there." Another said: "He will be missed, not because of the dollar. Because of what he gave me spiritually."

Father Dollar Bill loved the poor, and he looked forward to his weekly trips to give them a boost. "I love it," he said. "God has given me the happiest part of my life at the end."

For if the eagerness is there, the gift is acceptable according to what one has. (2 Corinthians 8:12)

God, may we never undervalue small acts of generosity.

The Angel Karly Foundation

Most parents think of each of their children as angels, gifts from God. But not many parents have babies born with "Angelman Syndrome," named after the doctor who first discovered this neuro-genetic disease in 1965. Although these babies are unable to communicate with words and prone to epilepsy, their loving eyes and wriggling bodies convey their perpetual states of happiness.

Five-year-old Karly Ruiz of San Antonio, Texas, is one such "angel." Although her initial diagnosis was tough on her parents, Rolando and Araceli, they decided to take positive action.

In 2009, the Ruizes established the Angel Karly Foundation, a nonprofit organization intended to raise awareness and provide a sense of solidarity for families of children with Angelman's Syndrome. Araceli credits the foundation's success to her special daughter.

"She's a huge gift from God and was given to us for a reason," Araceli explained to *Today's Catholic* reporter Carol Baass Sowa. "God wanted us to do this—the foundation."

Every perfect gift is from above, coming down from the Father of lights. (James 1:17)

Abba, protect children, the purest of Your angels on Earth.

Helping Internet Addicts

The Internet has grown into both an invaluable source of information and an excellent means of communication. However, surfing the web is a pastime best done in moderation because it can lead to Internet addiction.

According to a recent Stanford University study cited in *The Catholic Moment*, one in eight Americans suffers from it.

To help youngsters overcome this addiction, a weekly cyber-support group was created at St. Thomas Aquinas Church, located on the campus of Indiana's Purdue University.

Parishioners Steve S. and Ken L. co-founded the ministry, which protects participants' anonymity. "I think pornography is a more obvious abuse," Ken L. observes, "but social media and gaming are abuse problems that many people are not aware of."

Steve S. adds, "I think we have created awareness that there is a problem. Will this have benefits in the future? That is up to God, not us."

Admitting you have a problem, to yourself and to God, is the first step to finally solving it.

Blessed is anyone who endures temptation. (James 1:12)

God, grant us the humility to overcome our addictions.

No Good Deed Goes Unrewarded

What would you do if you found $20,000 in cash? Bismark Mensah, a Walmart employee and Ghanaian immigrant in Seattle, was faced with this moral quandary when he found an envelope stuffed with $20,000 in an empty shopping cart. He had seen the customer using that cart, so he immediately ran after her to return the hefty amount of cash.

The couple the envelope belonged to, Leona Wisdom and Gary Elton, were planning to use the money for a down payment on a house. Wisdom had asked the bank for the money in bills because they didn't want to have to wait for the check to clear. Eyes filled with tears of joy and relief, Wisdom offered the conscientious Mensah a reward for his selfless act, an offer which he firmly but politely refused.

Mensah was, however, honored with an "Integrity in Action" award by his Walmart employers. According to the *Daily Mail,* he was also given a plaque for his "heroic actions." Mensah came to America to obtain a better education and job, as well as the means to send financial support to his struggling family in Africa. His integrity sets an example for everyone.

For we are...created...for good works.
(Ephesians 2:10)

Abba, guide us to perform unselfish deeds.

The Tweeting Nun

"A lightning bolt experience." That's how Sister Helena Burns described the calling to become a nun that she felt at age 15. She entered the convent at age 17, choosing the Daughters of St. Paul because of their focus on media.

Sister Helena told the *Chicago Catholic*, "I looked at a lot of communities, but I thought what better way to bring God into peoples' lives than through a book or song or magazine or film? You can very directly reach people on a deep level. It's an art—we are using these arts to communicate with people."

Not only is Sister Helena a regular presence on Facebook and Twitter, she is also working on a documentary about Father James Alberione, the founder of the Daughters of St. Paul.

She said, "We want [people] to know the life of this amazing media saint...to let them know that it is possible to have sanctity go together with the latest technology—not just for holy uses and pondering the word of God, but in our everyday lives."

Remember to include God in every aspect of your life.

Whatever you do, do everything for the glory of God. (1 Corinthians 10:31)

Inspire us to use technology wisely, Creator.

Celebrating Dads

In some circles, fathers get a bad rap, writes Carolina Pichardo in the *Manhattan Times*. Often it's men in urban areas who are viewed as poor role models.

Pichardo agrees there are serious issues to consider concerning absent fathers—for instance, socioeconomic status and educational attainment. But she focuses on the positive.

"We turn to many local fathers who defy such conventions and instead serve as great examples of the kind of parent whose focus is on the well-being of the children."

One Bronx dad was heartbroken and shocked when his son was diagnosed with autism. Nevertheless, says his wife, "he is a dedicated husband and father who really enjoys spending time with his family."

Another dad says, "Whenever I make a decision...I have a little voice reminding me, 'My daughter might see this; is it something she'll be proud of?'"

Celebrate fathers who are great role models.

**Know the God of your father, and serve Him with single mind and willing heart.
(1 Chronicles 28:9)**

Father in heaven, watch over fathers everywhere.

The World's Friendliest Restaurant

If you're looking for the world's friendliest restaurant, look no further than Tim's Place in Albuquerque, New Mexico. As 27-year-old owner Tim Harris told one reporter, they serve "breakfast, lunch and hugs, but hugs are the best part."

Harris is thought to be the United States' first restaurant owner with Down Syndrome. His parents always encouraged him to be independent, and didn't treat him any differently than they did his three brothers.

Harris worked at local restaurants as a teenager, becoming popular with patrons for his friendly and upbeat attitude. His mother told radio station *KRQE*, "He has this unique quality where he is happy literally every day."

After Harris finished food service and office skills programs at Eastern New Mexico University, his parents decided to buy him a restaurant so he could become financially self-sufficient. He now gets up at 5:30 every morning to work at a job he loves, and greet each diner with a smile—and a hug.

You are the salt of the earth. (Matthew 5:13)

Remind me that Your light is reflected in all people, Lord, regardless of ability or disability.

Healthy Habits

Adults try various strategies to encourage children to eat right and exercise often. Some methods work better than others.

Helen Butleroff-Leahy has a tactic that really sings...and dances. The former Rockette turned registered dietician engages New York City school kids and drama professionals in a production called *My Plate: The New Food Guide Musical.* She'd like to take her popular show national, according to the *New York Times.*

Enthusiastic kids (some dressed as vegetables) perform gymnastics, dance, and "proclaim the virtues of 'eating for the health of it.'" Audiences include parents and teachers, some struggling with their own poor eating habits. Many attendees absorb the intended message that good eating includes foods such as whole grains, vegetables, fruits and nuts.

Changing a bad habit to a good one takes willpower and determined effort, but isn't your health—be it physical or spiritual—worth it?

Health and fitness are better than any gold, and a robust body than countless riches. (Sirach 30:15)

Help us, Lord, to set realistic and achievable goals.

The Belgium-Hawaii Connection

One long-time link closed with the death of a priest in Hawaii last year—but another chapter opened at the same time, promising the continuation of a glorious mission tradition.

Father Stephen Van den Eynde passed away in February 2012 at the age of 90, the last in a chain of Belgian-born members of the Congregation of the Fathers and Brothers of the Sacred Hearts of Jesus and Mary to serve as missionaries in Hawaii. Their number includes the legendary St. Damien—Father Damien de Vuester, the "leper priest" of Molokai.

The Belgium-Hawaii connection came about in the mid-1800s when the French and Belgian groups of the Sacred Hearts Fathers divided their responsibilities; France sent its missioners to Tahiti and other islands, while the Belgians brought Hawaii under their wing. Most of the hundreds who went toiled in relative anonymity, helping to build the church in Hawaii.

At the same time, though, the Belgian priests worked to encourage local vocations. That part of their tradition goes forward, pointing to a new trend that will live on in the future.

Go into all the world and proclaim the Good News. (Mark 16:15)

Christ, enrich holy legacies in our world.

The Way To Heaven

"I hear music," murmured the patient as he was awaking from anesthesia after a serious operation.

"Oh, don't let that bother you," said his nurse. "That's just St. Peter's band."

"St. Peter's band?" sighed the sick man. "That means I made it! I made it!"

Realizing that her patient thought he had arrived at the pearly gates, the nurse quickly replied, "I'm so sorry, but that's just the band practicing at St. Peter's school across the street."

It would be a relief for any of us to feel that somewhere during our pilgrimage through life we could feel sure we had "made it," that we had come through the battle of life with flying colors and merited heaven's everlasting peace. But God has the final say about our entrances and exits on the stage of life.

Each of us must first complete the particular job He sent us here to do before we can report back to Him and say, "Mission accomplished."

Be faithful until death, and I will give you the crown of life. (Revelation 2:10)

Thank You, Lord, for allowing me to play a part in sanctifying the world.

Cancer Does Not Discriminate

When country music star and former *American Idol* contestant Kellie Pickler shaved off her long, blond hair, the purpose wasn't to make a fashion statement. Rather, she did it in support of her best friend, Summer Holt Miller, who was diagnosed with breast cancer at age 36.

With a family history of breast cancer, Miller knew the odds were high that she would get it too, so she asked her doctor for a mammogram when she felt a lump during a self-exam. Tests revealed a tumor, which led her to undergo a double mastectomy and endure chemotherapy treatments to prevent the cancer from coming back.

Miller shaved her hair off instead of letting it fall out slowly due to the chemo. In a show of solidarity, Pickler did the same. She also hoped that her decision would help others. She said, "Cancer does not discriminate. If this compels even one person to change their mentality toward waiting until the age of 40 for their mammogram, then it will be worth it."

Happily, Miller is now cancer free.

A friend loves at all times. (Proverbs 17:17)

Give those with cancer the strength to endure their suffering, Healing Savior.

Planting Seeds in Your Soul

In the book *New Seeds of Contemplation,* Trappist monk and author Thomas Merton offers the following thoughts about the seeds God plants in each of our lives:

"Every moment and every event of every man's life on earth plants something in his soul. For just as the wind carries thousands of winged seeds, so each moment brings with it germs of spiritual vitality that come to rest imperceptibly in the minds and wills of men. Most of these unnumbered seeds perish and are lost, because men are not prepared to receive them: for such seeds as these cannot spring up anywhere except in the good soil of freedom, spontaneity, and love…We must learn to realize that the love of God seeks us in every situation, and seeks our good. His inscrutable love seeks our awakening.

"If these seeds would take root in my liberty, and if His will would grow from my freedom, I would become the love that He is, and my harvest would be His glory and my own joy."

Now the Lord is the Spirit, and where the Spirit of the Lord is, there is freedom. (2 Corinthians 3:17)

Make me aware, Holy Spirit, of opportunities for spiritual growth.

The Shirt Off Your Back

Californian Darlene Stewart sent the following note into the Bakersfield Observed blog about an incident she witnessed in her hometown.

She wrote, "On a recent trip to the Oildale Post Office, I observed a man with no shirt (possibly homeless) asking directions to the morgue, because his brother had just died. He asked a couple driving out of the post office parking lot about directions to the morgue. They in turn asked me, and I directed them next door to Mish Funeral Home.

"The gentleman in the car, not wanting him to have to go into the funeral home without a shirt, took his shirt off and offered it to him but he did not want to accept it. The gentleman wouldn't take no for an answer and just slipped it over his head. This is the only time I have ever witnessed someone literally 'giving the shirt off his back.'"

Clothe yourselves with compassion, kindness, humility, meekness. (Colossians 3:12)

Make me sensitive to the immediate needs of the less fortunate, Compassionate Father.

Go West — to Greeley

"Go West, young man" wrote Horace Greeley as founding editor of the *New York Tribune* back in the mid-1800s. The man who championed western expansion would probably be delighted with the city in Colorado that bears his name.

Connie Willis, an award-winning science fiction writer, admits to a "love affair" with that very city. She speaks of the city's residents as "engaged."

As she writes every day at the Starbucks near the University of Northern Colorado campus, Willis finds the interaction with the diverse population—farmers and ranchers to Somali refugees, Rotary club members and realtors to college students—as enriching. Greeley, she says, is "just right."

No matter which direction our lives take, it's always a "best practice" to stop and live fully in each moment—with each person we meet.

I tell you, many will come from east and west and will eat with Abraham and Isaac and Jacob in the kingdom of heaven. (Matthew 8:11)

Guide my steps, Master; show me Your way.

"Star Wars" and Ash Wednesday

In the movie *Star Wars: A New Hope,* heroes Luke Skywalker and Han Solo escape from the Death Star in their spaceship, the Millennium Falcon, only to be pursued by the evil Empire.

When Luke shoots down his first enemy ship, he gets excited and yells, "I got him!"

Han, a veteran of space battles, responds, "Great, kid! Don't get cocky."

In a nutshell, that's also the message of Ash Wednesday.

When the priest puts ashes on our foreheads, he cites Genesis 3:19: "Remember, that you are dust, and unto dust you shall return." In other words: no matter what we accomplish on this earth, no matter how powerful we are, no matter how much cash we have in the bank, our physical bodies will eventually all meet the same end. Therefore, we need to live the best life possible in the knowledge that "God so loved the world that He gave His only Son, so that everyone who believes in Him might not perish but might have eternal life."

That's great news! But don't get cocky.

The arrogant do not endure. (Habakkuk 2:5)

Jesus, help me give up all that separates me from You.

The Purpose of Lent

With its emphasis on penance and sacrifice, the season of Lent can seem disruptive to our lives. According to writer Kerry Weber, that's the way it's supposed to be.

She said, "Lent itself can sometimes seem to be little more than a checklist of things to do or not do...I find myself wondering: How am I supposed to live a normal life while doing all of these 'extra' things for Lent? The short answer is: I'm not.

"Lent is meant to...push us outside of our comfort zones. Lent is a time of preparation, of purification. But while all my lists are well-intended, it's all too easy to lose sight of their larger purpose, and to forget what, exactly, I'm trying to prepare for.

"Lent is meant to help us recognize and identify with the suffering of others, to consider others' needs before our own—and one doesn't do that simply by crossing items off a list. [Taking part] in the Lenten traditions of prayer, fasting, and almsgiving are not meant to distract from, but be enhancements to our everyday life. They open us up to be more loving, more giving."

Grow in the grace and knowledge of our...Savior. (2 Peter 3:18)

Increase my ability to imitate Your love, Lord.

An Earthquake's Lesson

The major earthquake that shook San Francisco on April 18, 1906, was also felt in nearby Oakland where eight-year-old Dorothy Day had recently moved with her parents and siblings. When the ground finally stopped shaking, a frightened Day emerged from her home to see examples of both chaos and community: buildings swayed, small fires burned, and adults calmed down scared children.

In her autobiography *The Long Loneliness,* Day—who would go on to found The Catholic Worker movement—admits she felt comforted by the sight of people helping one another. She wrote, "While the crisis lasted, people loved each other. It was as though they were united in Christian solidarity. It makes one think of how people could, if they would, care for each other in times of stress, unjudgingly in pity and love."

Don't let times of tragedy and stress be the only occasions when you feel united with loved ones and strangers. Open yourself to that kind of love and caring on a daily basis.

I want their hearts to be encouraged and united in love. (1 Colossians 2:2)

Jesus, unite all people in Christian solidarity.

Band of Angels

They called them the "Band of Angels," and few titles hit the mark as much as that one. They were the military nurses—66 from the Army and 11 from the Navy—who were stationed in the Philippines in the early days of World War II and served out their time in harsh detainment camps after they were taken prisoner. There they continued to nurse wounded, dying and disease-ridden troops, earning their release only when they were liberated by Allied forces in 1945.

When Mildred Manning died last March at the age of 98, she was the lone survivor of the Band of Angels. She joined the Army Nurse Corps in 1939 to see the world, but as she was later to remark, "And what I saw was a prison camp."

The prison experience would mark her life, but she said, "Our internment was nothing compared to the Bataan Death March and imprisonment our soldiers went through. They were tortured and starved." Still she viewed her detainment as something positive. "If I could survive that," she said, "I could survive anything."

You...have stood by me in my trials. (Luke 22:28)

Paraclete, help us to endure trials with resilience.

Homeless Man's Helping Hand

On the surface, Curtis Jackson was a typical homeless man who walked up and down Chicago's streets, begging for money. What made Jackson so extraordinary was that the money he collected wasn't for him. It was for his jobless friend, a 39-year-old woman who remains anonymous.

She had been employed at a bank, and would often provide Jackson with food at her home. But in 2011, she lost both her job and her home.

When the Department of Children and Family Services threatened to take away her 10-year-old son if she couldn't find them a place to live, Jackson knew it was time to act. "I'm out here for a purpose: to help someone," he told reporter Daniel Bates about his charitable work. "And once she doesn't need help anymore, I'll move on to someone else."

In five months, Jackson raised $9,000 for his friend. Words could not adequately express her gratitude. "Thank God that we did have an angel waiting for us," she declared.

Comfort your hearts and strengthen them in every good work. (2 Thessalonians 2:17)

Father, help us to always give generously of our time.

Enough is Enough

It wasn't all that long ago—51 years, to be exact. That was when Baltimore's Cardinal Lawrence Shehan decided that he'd had enough of the de facto segregation that existed between blacks and whites, and issued an uncompromising pastoral letter on racial justice in March, 1963. It would set a national standard.

"Our Christian faith imposes upon us all a special duty of both justice and charity toward all men, no matter what may be their racial and social origin," he wrote. "It must guide us in our personal relationships...within our block, our neighborhood, our community, in our social and fraternal organizations; in the business we may conduct; in the labor unions to which we may belong; at work and at play; in all the circumstances of everyday life."

Racially, things were very different then, but there's still a lot of work to be done. All people have the example of Cardinal Shehan to help them chart a course of action. His secret? He simply decided that enough was enough—and took it from there.

Speak out for those who cannot speak, for the rights of all the destitute. (Proverbs 31:8)

Father, bless our efforts, big and small, to promote justice.

Pride Shouldn't Be a Barrier

Diagnosed with Stage IV gastrointestinal cancer at age 38, the late Lt. Col. Mark Weber recalled a formative experience about enduring suffering with dignity and grace when he was a teen. He helped care for his grandmother who was confined to a wheelchair after a stroke and couldn't move half her body.

During an interview on *Christopher Closeup* about his memoir *Tell My Sons,* Weber said, "I took this woman to the bathroom. She weighed 160 pounds; I weighed maybe 130. I had to take her underwear down and help her in every borderline undignified way. But there was no lost dignity. For me to be able to take care of her felt comforting."

Weber believes his grandmother's example helped him deal with his own periods of debilitation. "When I can't do something, I find it much easier to accept offers of assistance," he said. "Pride is not a barrier for me."

Asking for help when you need it isn't a sign of weakness. God wants us to rely on Him and the people He put into our lives. Be humble enough to accept that support.

He gave help to all the humble.
(1 Maccabees 14:14)

Prevent pride from being a barrier to love, Redeemer.

Moving Beyond Rejection

Born with Down Syndrome, Diana Braun endured rejection not only from society, but from her own mother. Placed into a state-run nursing home in Freeport, Illinois, at age eight, she grew up determined to be an advocate for people with disabilities.

At age 19, Braun began a friendship with Kathy Conour, who had cerebral palsy and required a lot of physical assistance. They were both determined to strike out on their own, so they decided to live independently—together.

Though Braun officially became Conour's personal caretaker, they relied on each other for support, learning to shop and manage household finances. They also worked to establish or maintain rights for people with disabilities, earning the Illinois Human Rights Award in 2005, and becoming the subjects of a film called *Body and Soul: Diana and Kathy.*

Though Conour died in 2009, Braun continues being a voice for the disabled—and a testament to the fact that every person has the God-given potential to accomplish great things.

Let us love one another. (2 John 1:5)

Help us be sources of encouragement to others, Jesus.

Keeping the Flame of Life Burning

At a recent church service in India, seminarian Praveen Lakkisetti had the opportunity to witness the ordination of three of his classmates. The bishop presiding over this ordination gave an inspiring sermon, proclaiming: "Today, more than ever, the church and the world needs priests—the praying priests."

After the ceremony, Lakkisetti thought about what why it is important to be a "praying priest" in today's fast-paced society. "A priest cannot give what he does not possess himself," he mused in *Today's Catholic*. "The primary task of a priest is to be a model of prayer and lead the people to drink abundantly from the spiritual wellsprings."

In a sense, Lakkisetti's observations can be applied to anyone, not just members of the clergy. Each of us needs to make prayer an integral part of our lives so we can nourish our own spirits, and be another Christ to those around us.

As Lakkisetti concludes, "Prayer is the wax that keeps the flame of life burning."

You are my lamp, O Lord, the Lord lightens my darkness. (2 Samuel 22:29)

Abba, may we be fervent and faithful in our daily prayers.

Barefoot for a Purpose

It is said that you should never judge someone until you've walked a mile in their shoes. Six years ago, Roberto Santiago—a parishioner at Portland, Oregon's Holy Family parish—took this saying literally when he chose to start walking everywhere barefoot in an effort to see how the less fortunate live.

"It's just a very small act of solidarity," Santiago told *The Catholic Sentinel*. "It gives me a little bit of a way to stay connected and be appreciative for what I have."

Santiago realizes that, unlike the poor, he has a house and a warm shower to come home to at the end of the day. But the goals of his barefoot endeavor are twofold.

"Personally, he sees it as a reminder to be ever thankful and humble," wrote Clarice Keating in *Catholic News Service*. "Publicly, he hopes his message helps raise awareness about the abject poverty experienced by people in developing countries."

If you have a calling or mission, however unusual, take Santiago's advice and just "do it." God will reward your efforts.

Be all the more eager to confirm your call. (2 Peter 1:10)

Jesus, infuse us with loving and empathetic spirits.

Children, Bodies and Souls

Even though children can't see their souls, it's present in everything they do, from brushing their teeth to running a race to showing love to their family, friends and God.

The Christopher Award-winning children's picture book *Forever You* teaches kids about this invisible yet eternal part of themselves that makes them human—and how they should always keep it in mind when making choices. Author Nicole Lataif told the Pauline Kids website what she hopes the book communicates to children and their parents:

"The most important take-away for children from this book is to understand that their bodies and souls are meant to express and communicate the love of Christ, and that they can choose to do this. Children should also identify their gifts and talents to begin to think about how God made them unique…Adults should ask themselves if they strive to live a virtuous life in Christ, or if they play by their own rules. In the words of Robert Fulghum, 'Don't worry that your children will never listen to you; worry that they are always watching you.'"

Train children in the right way. (Proverbs 22:6)

Guide children and parents toward virtuous lives, Father.

Mr. Baseball's Second Chance

Named California's "Mr. Baseball" in 2010 while a senior at Santa Ana's Mater Dei High School, Cory Hahn was on the road to fulfilling his dream of becoming a professional baseball player. But one week into his freshman season with Arizona State University, Hahn's head-first slide into a second baseman's leg left him paralyzed for life from the mid-chest down.

While in the hospital, the president of the Arizona Diamondbacks, Derrick Hall, visited Hahn and left impressed with the young man's passion for and knowledge of the game. He was impressed even more by Hahn's return to school as a student and his striving toward a degree of independence.

In June 2013, the Arizona Diamondbacks picked Cory Hahn in the 34th round of the Major League Baseball draft. Though he won't be a player, they plan to give him a job with the organization. Hahn shared on Twitter that he is "humbled" and "grateful" for the opportunity. His previously shattered dream of a baseball career has taken on a new life in a new way.

Be patient in suffering; persevere in prayer. (Romans 12:12)

Guide us down new roads when our dreams are broken, Father.

Hope on St. Patrick's Day

The late Father Andrew Greeley once penned this Irish Blessing:

"May your hope be...
As determined as the river racing by,
As soft as the cry of the mourning dove,
As sweet and subtle as a lover's sigh,...
As resolute as the sun rising each day,
As certain as the return each year of spring.
May it break through the darkling clouds
And confirm you against every evil thing.
May Jesus and Mary and Patrick and Brigid
Strengthen your faith and hope and love,
And may God bless you...
Father, Son and Holy Spirit."

Why are you cast down, O my soul, and why are you disquieted within me? Hope in God; for I shall again praise Him, my help. (Psalm 42:5)

May hope always reside in my heart, Redeemer, and may I pass that spirit of hope on to others.

A Day's Little Joys

Blogger Lori Deschene advocates for simple pleasures throughout a day. "When you connect the dots between all these little joys," she writes, "life seems fuller and more satisfying."

Here are some items on her list of "little things that can make a big difference" in a day.

- A smile from a stranger; give one and you may get one in return.
- An outdoor lunch. Nothing feels better than sunlight!
- Passing a park and seeing children at play, or playing a game you loved as a child.
- A long phone conversation. Call an old friend, and "remember when."
- Something so funny it makes you laugh out loud.
- A beautiful sunset or sunrise.

In every moment of every day, remembering God loves us is cause for boundless joy.

Let all who take refuge in You rejoice; let them ever sing for joy. (Psalm 5:11)

Fill my heart with Your love, Lord, to share with neighbors near and far.

Being a Protector

During his papal installation Mass on March 19, 2013—also the Feast of St. Joseph—Pope Francis cited what we can learn from the man whom God chose to raise Jesus, His Son.

Pope Francis said, "How does Joseph respond to his calling to be the protector of Mary, Jesus and the Church? By being constantly attentive to God, open to the signs of God's presence and receptive to God's plans, and not simply to his own."

The Pope continued, "Joseph is a 'protector' because he is able to hear God's voice and be guided by His will; and for this reason he is all the more sensitive to the persons entrusted to his safekeeping. He can look at things realistically, he is in touch with his surroundings, he can make truly wise decisions. In him, dear friends, we learn how to respond to God's call, readily and willingly, but we also see the core of the Christian vocation, which is Christ! Let us protect Christ in our lives, so that we can protect others, so that we can protect creation!"

For all who are led by the Spirit of God are children of God. (Romans 8:14)

Heavenly Redeemer, help us to be more sensitive to Your call in our lives.

A Car Crashes Into Your House

Chances are you'd be furious if a car came crashing through your house because the driver forgot to set the emergency brake. For Tom Peterson—founder of the evangelization ministry Catholics Come Home and author of a book with the same title—that wasn't just a hypothetical situation, but a lived experience.

Friends who were staying at his family's summer home in Flagstaff, Arizona, called to tell him that a car had crashed through the front of the house. A high school girl, who had parked her car on a hill, neglected to set the parking brake. Thankfully, no one was hurt. When Peterson arrived at the accident scene, the tearful high school student and her mother were sincerely apologetic.

Instead of losing his temper (which he would have done had the incident happened two weeks prior), Peterson forgave the girl. She was shocked, so he told her that he'd recently been on a retreat where he had a life-changing experience of Jesus' love and mercy. He extended the same forgiveness to her that Jesus extends to all of us.

Pray for the grace to be as forgiving as Jesus.

**Blessed be...the Father of mercies.
(2 Corinthians 1:3)**

Help me be a model of mercy, Holy Spirit.

Help on the Final Journey

Calvary Hospital in the Bronx, New York, is known for treating terminally ill patients, but a visitor would hardly suspect it. There's an air of love and serenity about the facility, typically reflected in a caring staff. That's certainly the case with Theresa "Terry" Mullins, a nurse who's a former New York City cop, and who was profiled last year in New York's *Daily News*.

Mullins tends to her patients at the St. Vincent de Paul residence in the Bronx, one of several hospices operated in the area by Calvary. "You come into people's lives for a very short time," she said. "You have very important work to do within a timeframe that is sometimes as short as a week."

Mullins relies on her former occupations (she was also a flight attendant) in helping put patients and their families at ease in difficult situations. "The patients are tired; they're fine with leaving this world," she said. "They're on a journey, and we have to help them complete it."

Blessed be the God...who consoles us in all our affliction, so that we may be able to console. (2 Corinthians 1:3,4)

Holy Physician, strengthen all healers.

Books to Soldiers

One New York teenager's initiative has resulted in U.S. soldiers in America and overseas receiving 20,000 free books.

Near the start of her freshman year at Ardsley High School in Westchester County, Jamie Stein was talking to her physical therapist, a former Marine who had recently served in the Middle East. He mentioned that books were a valuable commodity to the servicemen and women there because it provides them with an escape from their stressful work and living situations.

A book lover herself, Stein started asking local libraries for book donations. Other people and organizations soon offered support as well. Stein and her mother deliver their donations to local Army bases for distribution overseas or to VA hospitals.

Stein, now a senior, told New York's *Daily News*, "[The project] has given me another look at how soldiers can affect us as a nation. They are heroes to us overseas, and it's really important to recognize that and give back to them."

Kudos to Jamie Stein for finding a unique way to offer words of support to members of the military.

Read from the book of the Lord. (Isaiah 34:16)

Inspire writers and readers, Holy Spirit.

She Was a Doozy

She was a whirlwind, a human dynamo. Even a "doozy," as one bishop—with deep admiration—once called her. Whatever she was, Mary Mulholland got things done, almost always for other people. She died last year at 85, and at her funeral in Morristown, New Jersey, mourners paid tribute to her lifetime of service to those in need—the poor, the suffering, the addicted.

For one thing, Mulholland started something called the Dope Open back in 1968. When it had run its course after 42 years, it stood as the most successful charity golf tournament in New Jersey history. It raised over $15 million, and the money went for drug and alcohol victims, battered women, domestic violence programs, and information sessions about AIDS.

That was only the beginning, though. Mulholland helped to build three hospitals, founded an agency for Catholic Charities, and brought in funds for cancer victims. In all, she personally raised more than $50 million for the charities she supported.

One person can indeed make a difference—and Mary Mulholland certainly did.

Faith by itself, if it has no works, is dead. (James 2:17)

Messiah, may our deeds reflect the fervor of our faith.

The Messy Quest for Meaning

Stephen Martin grew up in a large, devout Catholic family, but like a lot of young people, he never thought about what his faith meant to him and why he believed what he did. After reading books during his high school years by famous writers who opposed religion, Martin followed their logic and doubted everything he'd been taught about God.

During an interview on *Christopher Closeup* about his book *The Messy Quest for Meaning,* Martin said he started asking himself, "Why are there so many problems in the world? How could a good God allow these things to exist?"

It wasn't until Martin lost his faith that he realized he also lost his sense of meaning and purpose and order in the world: "When I forfeited that, just voluntarily walked away from it, I saw how important it is to have a spiritual compass in your life. Because from the end of high school all through college, I was very directionless."

More of the story tomorrow…

I have gone astray like a lost sheep; seek out Your servant. (Psalm 119:176)

Guide all the spiritually lost back to You, Good Shepherd.

Breaking Through Life's Clutter

The seeds of a renewed faith got planted in Stephen Martin during a conversation with his uncle, a priest. Martin, who was attending Duke University at the time, lamented the fact that his fellow student, all-star basketball player Bobby Hurley, got all the breaks and talent in life. In comparing himself to Hurley, Martin felt jealous, like he didn't measure up and never would.

Martin's uncle told him that God distributes different talents to everyone. Instead of worrying about what talents he didn't have, he should look harder for the ones he did have and how to use them. That wisdom was lost on Martin at the time, but stayed with him as he matured.

Still feeling somewhat lost, Martin developed a severe anxiety disorder that led to a mental breakdown. Though it was traumatic at the time, he now sees that experience as a blessing, as God breaking through the clutter in his life. It forced him to slow down and figure out better ways to live.

The conclusion of the story tomorrow.

Serve one another with whatever gift each of you has received. (1 Peter 4:10)

Help me appreciate the talents You've given me, Creator.

Creating a Virtuous Cycle

While recovering from his breakdown, Stephen Martin adopted a physically and spiritually healthier lifestyle. He started going to church regularly with his girlfriend (and now wife) Dawn, making time for daily prayer, and pursuing five practices he'd learned on his winding faith journey.

He details these practices in his book *The Messy Quest for Meaning*, but explained them in brief during his *Christopher Closeup* interview:

"Figure out what your strengths are, what your passions are. Then you need the focus and the structure to take those passions and channel them. You need humility to know what your strengths and weaknesses are. You need a sense of community, so you've got other people helping you understand what your strengths and weaknesses are…There's a fifth practice I call 'margins.' This is about taking a leap in some area of your life, really stretching yourself. I think when you get all five of these things working, it creates a virtuous cycle."

I came that they may have life, and have it more abundantly. (John 10:10)

Help me to move beyond self-limiting boundaries, Lord.

The Unforgettables

In 2011, researcher Dr. Mary Mittelman created The Unforgettables, a chorus made up of Alzheimer's patients and their spouses, in association with the NYU Langone School of Medicine. The purpose: to study if music had any impact on memory loss or dementia. Results so far are promising.

Dr. Mittelman told the *Daily News* that she doesn't claim her work has slowed down the participants' illnesses—that would need an official study—but she does believe the social interaction and brain stimulation improves their lives. Lin Jacobson, whose husband Manny is a participant, said rehearsals and concerts are "two hours of sheer joy for both of us."

Conductor Tania Papayannopoulou adds, "There is a lot of isolation and depression that comes with this disease. Our group is so united, they have all made friends. They may not remember everything we have taught from week to week, but they can sing the songs…and look into their partner's eyes and feel the love they have for each other. It's just gorgeous to see."

With gratitude in your hearts sing psalms, hymns, and spiritual songs. (Colossians 3:16)

May music comfort the afflicted, Healing Savior.

Amigos for Christ

Donating money to charities is always appreciated, but when it comes to non-profit organizations, actions speak louder than words. The Our Lady of Providence students and teachers from Clarksville, Indiana, who volunteered to help Amigos for Christ in Nicaragua, learned this important lesson firsthand.

Orchestrated by the school's Spanish teacher, Alan Matthews, this mission trip was meant to inspire pupils to do more "hands-on service."

"Giving money is something everyone wants to do, but there's something about reaching out," Matthews explained to *The Criterion*. With assistance from these Providence students, the Amigos for Christ installed a pipeline that allowed poor villages access to clean water.

"The work that Amigos for Christ does permanently changes the lives of all the people who live in these communities," Providence graduate Elliott Happel observed. "It also changes the lives of the people who were able to give them this new life."

The needy shall not always be forgotten. (Psalm 9:18)

God, may our good intentions be defined by actions, not just words.

A Conduit to the Light of God

Author Dawn Eden grew up in what she calls a "sexually porous household." As she explained on *Christopher Closeup,* "I wasn't sheltered from adults' nudity or substance abuse or sex talk." In addition, she was sexually abused by a janitor at a temple her mother sometimes attended.

All these experiences left Eden emotionally scarred because "children do tend to blame themselves for the evils committed against them." She finally began to deal with the mental and emotional fallout of the abuse after her conversion to Christianity as an adult. She has written a book called *My Peace I Give You: Healing Sexual Wounds with the Help of the Saints* to share her insights with other abuse victims.

Eden said, "I've actively sought to learn how I can help others through my wounds. These were wounds that I used to feel guilt and shame about, which I now realize is misplaced guilt and shame. So for me, being able to bring these wounds into the light of Christ has been very healing. It's also been a joy to be able to ask God how He can use my pain to help others."

He heals the brokenhearted. (Psalm 147:3)

Heal our inner and outer infirmities, Divine Physician.

Following God's Lead

Putting ourselves in God's hands requires giving up a degree of control in our lives. According to Tim Muldoon, author of *The Ignatian Workout: Daily Spiritual Exercises for a Healthy Faith,* that surrender can bring unexpected rewards.

Muldoon writes, "The single most common mistake people make in their spiritual lives is wanting *God* to follow *their* lead. ...If we want to take God seriously, though, we must be the ones ready to follow *God's* lead."

Muldoon concludes, "Initial reticence to pay attention to God's invitation is not uncommon, for His call pulls us outside of the comfort zones we create for ourselves in a scary world. [But] as scary as it is, it is about trusting that God wants our ultimate good and believing that God is more capable than we are of leading us to it...The fundamental posture of authentic prayer...is that of openness to the will of God for our lives, for it is through that will that we will be led to our very reason for existing in the first place."

See how good it is to follow the Lord. (Sirach 46:10)

Increase my trust in You, Heavenly Father.

I've Got to Do Something

From his home in Evansville, Indiana, Stan Gregory watched coverage of Hurricane Sandy as it walloped coastal areas of New York and New Jersey. Seeing the devastation, he said to his wife: "I've got to do something." Her reply: "Pack your bags." So that's exactly what Stan Gregory did.

Loading a truck with food from a local church, he began driving east and ended up in Little Ferry, New Jersey. A relief worker there told him they weren't set up at that point to help the victims, but Gregory would not be deterred.

"I've got pork chops in that truck," he said, "and I'm going to grill them in New Jersey somewhere tonight." So he started grilling—and fed about 150 people before the food ran out. Local merchants pitched in to help next, and before Gregory headed home three days later, he had served about 2,000 meals.

The town would honor him with a citation and a standing ovation, and for Gregory, that was reward enough. "This experience is the greatest thing that ever happened to me," he said. "I got to touch people's hearts."

Open your hand to the poor.
(Deuteronomy 15:11)

Lord, the best gift we can give to others is our time.

Leave 'Em Laughing...and Thinking

If used properly, funny stories can be great moral teachers. Auxiliary Bishop Christopher J. Coyne of Indianapolis observes in *The Criterion,* "Humor in a homily is a means to an end. It should always serve the Catholic message the preacher is trying to communicate."

Monsignor Joseph Schaedel, pastor of St. Luke the Evangelist Church in Indianapolis, agrees and remembers some sage counsel he received from Archbishop Emeritus Daniel M. Buechlein: "He always said a preacher should not attempt to use humor unless he's the kind of person who jokes around anyway."

The good-humored Msgr. Schaedel added, "I recently used humor to make a point about people thinking the grass is always greener for someone else. I told how a single lady put an ad in the paper. It said, 'Husband wanted.' She got 300 replies, and they all said the same thing: 'You can have mine.'"

According to Msgr. Schaedel and other humorously inclined clergymen, the key is not to let the heart of their sermons get buried beneath too many jokes. These priests always hope for their parishioners to learn even as they laugh.

There is...a time to laugh. (Ecclesiastes 3:1,4)

May our lives be filled with laughter and wisdom in Christ.

Softening a Hardened Heart

Frank Weathers swore that he would never forgive his father for divorcing his mother. It had happened when Frank was five. The elder Weathers admitted that decision was the biggest mistake of his life, and hoped for his son's forgiveness. But Frank never gave it—until he converted to Catholicism.

Writing on his Patheos.com blog, Frank recalled inviting his father to his home in 2008. After beating around the bush for a while, he finally told him, "Dad, I just want you to know that I forgive you for leaving us." His father replied, "Son, I really needed to hear that from you. I am so sorry." Tears were shed.

Frank concluded, "I firmly believe that this never would have happened if I hadn't become a Catholic. If I hadn't been praying the Liturgy of the Hours, where the psalms worked on softening my hardened heart to prepare me for this moment. If I hadn't been saying the Lord's Prayer daily, saying the words 'forgive us our trespasses, as we forgive those who trespass against us.' It became a call to action, you see. What good does it do to say the words, but not to do what they say?"

Forgive, and you will be forgiven. (Luke 6:37)

Grant me the grace to forgive those who've hurt me, Lord.

Saved by a Kayaker

On Thursday, April 4, 2013, an SUV carrying a family of five plummeted off the edge of a steep cliff and into the American River in Northern California. The car fell where Mark Devittorio had been floating inside his kayak just seconds before.

"It's fortuitous that they didn't actually land on me," Devittorio told *KCRA-TV*.

Devittorio quickly jumped out of his kayak and rescued the three children, bringing them to shore. When he swam back to retrieve their parents, he discovered the driver, Christian Lemler, whose wife was holding his head above water. "He wanted to live," Devittorio said of Lemler. "He wanted to be with his family."

Thanks to Devittorio and the El Dorado County Fire Department, who happened to be close by at the time, the Lemler family was saved.

Guardian angels can come in all shapes and sizes. May God's blessings visit each and every one.

The angel of the Lord encamps around those who fear Him, and delivers them. (Psalm 34:7)

Abba, bless and protect the Good Samaritans of our world.

Through the Eyes of Service

The death of their son Francis turned the LaHood family around. The LaHoods not only mourned Francis, who died in 1988 after living just a few minutes, but gradually came to devote themselves to other children with disabilities. Today their modest home in Silver Spring, Maryland, is filled with as many as eight disabled children, and their altruistic calling has become more than just a ministry—it's their life's work.

It's a calling that involves Dan LaHood and his wife, Cubby, on a full-time basis, and their other children as well. They receive no government funding or money from the Washington Archdiocese, but rely entirely on donations and the grants generated by a board of directors. And Dan LaHood? He gave up his own job to care for children with special needs, and he couldn't be happier.

He says, "I've learned when you love someone you see them with new eyes...the eyes of service. And it really does make you happy. Maybe that's the biggest change. I'm happy now in a way I never could have imagined."

Be...eager to confirm your call. (2 Peter 1:10)

Christ, may we be open to Your guiding Spirit in our lives.

New Home for Wounded Warrior

Private First Class Semisi Tokailagi is smiling in the photo published last summer by New York's *Daily News*. He and his wife, Miriama, were preparing to move into a new home that was all theirs, courtesy of the Military Warriors Support Foundation. The organization provides housing to service members wounded in combat, and thanks to an arrangement with the Bank of America, it's all mortgage-free.

Tokailagi was seriously wounded in 2011 during a rocket attack in Afghanistan. After he awoke from a month-long coma, he underwent treatment for several months in military hospitals and received the Purple Heart for his bravery. Then the Military Warriors heard about him and went to work.

The Tokailagis' new two-story home is in the Harding Park section of the Bronx, New York, a working-class community where neighbors were there to welcome them. One resident described the neighborhood as "like family." Added Edwin Rivera, who will live next door to the Tokailagis, "We want them to feel welcome. And to know that we appreciate his service."

**Love your neighbor as yourself.
(Leviticus 19:18)**

God, may we extend a hand in friendship to others.

Caring for Special People

Faith and fellowship are the cornerstones of the Faith and Life movement, established in France in 1971 by Jean Vanier and now reaching into 80 different countries. Vanier is also founder of the L'Arche community, which works worldwide with the intellectually disabled, and with which Faith and Life is loosely affiliated. One chapter in the Twin Cities of St. Paul and Minneapolis was recently profiled in *The Catholic Spirit*.

"It's getting together and having these special people have some fun" along with sharing opportunities for prayer and singing, said Mary Jeanne Hemesath, the leader of the group.

One of the "special people" the group works with, Kathleen Sweeney, gave it her ringing endorsement. "I like to be here," said Sweeney, who attended a session with her father, Jim. "It makes me feel good. I make friends."

As expressed by Hemesath, that's what Faith and Life is all about. "Our Lord gave us these special people to take care of," she said. "And He did it for a reason."

When you give a banquet, invite the poor, the crippled...And you will be blessed. (Luke 14:13-14)

Jesus, may we lovingly care for those with special needs.

Happiness and Meaning

Do you want to live a happy life or a meaningful life? Though there's overlap between the two, a recent study in the *Journal of Positive Psychology* reveals they're more different than you might think. As summarized in *The Atlantic* magazine, psychologists found that a happy life is "associated with being a 'taker' while a meaningful life corresponds with being a 'giver.'"

Meaning, according to researchers, stems from transcending yourself, from actively seeking out the good of others even when it requires sacrifice on your part. Happiness, on the other hand, is more self-focused. It arises from satisfying your own desires and experiencing a minimal amount of stress.

Kathleen Vohs, one of the study's authors, explains, "Happy people get a lot of joy from receiving benefits from others while people leading meaningful lives get a lot of joy from giving to others."

Though we all want to be happy, maybe we could add a little more meaning to our lives as well. That choice can help us create a better world—and better connect our souls with Christ.

The Son of Man came...to serve. (Mark 10:45)

Help me derive joy from helping others, Jesus.

A Lifetime of Redemption

Throughout the Bible, the limits of God's mercy know no bounds. He pardons the transgressions of tax collectors, prostitutes and thieves, to name a few. One of the most significant portraits of a penitent sinner drawn in the Scriptures is that of the former adulteress who kneels at Jesus' feet, baptizing them with tears and costly perfume.

According to *Catholic News Service* writer Allan F. Wright, we should look to this woman's humble example when laying our own sins before God. "What may we need to 'pour out' at the feet of Jesus?" he asks. "Which actions, omissions, attitudes? Like the sinful woman, when we 'pour out' our sins in the confessional, we experience the forgiveness of Christ."

There is no greater freedom for us as Christians than the release from the entanglements of our sins, which seek to separate us from God. But as Wright says, we must be as sincere in our remorse as the repentant woman was. Only then can we hope to experience true oneness with Jesus.

If we confess our sins, He...will forgive us...and cleanse us from all unrighteousness. (1 John 1:9)

Messiah, may we never neglect the act of confession.

To Know the Poor

On the way home from visiting a college campus with her daughter, Effie Caldarola of Omaha stopped to give the remains of their leftover pizza to a homeless man.

"The episode sticks in my mind because I wonder why we didn't, on a safe block on a busy street, take the time to offer a little conversation with our meager gift?" Caldarola muses. She then considers the example Jesus set by not only reaching out to help the poor, but taking the time to get to know them.

"In an *Omaha World Herald* story, columnist Erin Grace tells of a man who decided on his 50th birthday to do something radical," Caldarola continued. "He's giving $50 away each week of his 50th year. We're not talking about writing 52 checks and patting himself on the back. No, he's personally handing $50 to mostly strangers whom he happens to encounter."

Caldarola recommends that we as Christians should also strive to emulate Christ's example, not just giving money to the impoverished but giving of ourselves, and of our time.

Give a hearing to the poor, and return their greeting politely. (Sirach 4:8)

Lord, may we never neglect the needs of those less fortunate.

Give Me A Chance

For many people, all they need is an opportunity to prove that they can succeed. Give Me a Chance, Inc., is an organization that, as its name suggests, offers women of Ogden, Utah, "a chance to learn basic skills and earn money to support their families." These skills range from mathematics to sewing.

Sister Maria Nguyen, the director of Give Me a Chance, Inc., founded the establishment three years ago. She first got the notion as a volunteer at Catholic Community Services, where she saw many immigrant women struggling to feed their children.

"Instead of just coming here [CCS] to wait, how about they do something for themselves?" Sister Maria mused to the *Intermountain Catholic* of Salt Lake City.

Give Me A Chance, Inc. has already produced one encouraging success story. A woman who has been with them from the beginning was promoted to head seamstress at the DeMarillac Boutique in Ogden. "What she learned from us is not only sewing skills," Sister Maria concluded. "She learned self-esteem."

The plans of the diligent lead...to abundance. (Proverbs 21:5)

Father, reward all honest efforts or work in Your Name.

Lord, Help Me Get Through This Day

Janet Kreiner of Manheim Township, Pennsylvania, hasn't slowed down even though she's now 73. But when she woke on Easter morning with a horrible twinge in her back, she feared she'd have to cancel her plans. She prayed, "Lord, help me get through this day."

Kreiner attended Mass, and afterwards, served sweets and stuffed animals to small children at the Catholic Worker House's annual community Easter dinner. The meals are served to more than 300 people who aren't able to have a home-cooked dinner regularly.

"As long as the Lord gives you two hands and two feet and a heart, you use them to do His work," Kreiner told *Lancaster Online News*. "That's why we're here—to do His work…Those of us who have need to share with those who have not."

By early afternoon, Kreiner realized her back pain was completely gone. In serving God and her neighbors, she found healing.

You shall worship the Lord your God, and I will bless your bread and your water; and I will take sickness away from among you. (Exodus 23:25)

Lord, help us give more of our time, energy, resources and love to those in need!

Towards a Better, Brighter Future

With little income and no support from her unborn child's father, Amanda searched for a place to live that would accommodate her and her baby. That's when she discovered Zechariah House in Parma, Ohio. It's a faith-based facility that's an offshoot of a program called Maggie's Place in Phoenix, Arizona. They offer housing and hospitality to expectant and young mothers who are homeless.

The facility's regional director, Tricia Kuivinen, told *The Cleveland Plain Dealer,* "The aim is to ensure [women] have a healthy delivery while keeping themselves healthy. From that point on, we help to instill self-sufficiency, like getting your GED, going to job-training classes...and other life skills that most of us take for granted. Those are big steps for young women who are looking for a better, brighter future."

Amanda, who manages a fast food restaurant while Ryan is in daycare, admits life can be challenging at times. But she is grateful for the family atmosphere at Zechariah House: "I'm lucky to have found such a caring place for my baby and me."

**Come in, my daughter, and welcome.
(Tobit 11:17)**

Guide us toward creating a culture of life, Divine Savior.

Money versus Honor

In his bestselling memoir *Big Russ and Me,* the late *NBC* newsman Tim Russert recalled a time when his father, a foreman with the South Buffalo Sanitation Department, qualified for a promotion. Securing the position would have meant a significant raise for a man with a family to support. Big Russ, as Russert's father was called, didn't get that promotion, but it wasn't until years later that his son discovered why.

Big Russ revealed that he was approached by three superiors who asked him to remove himself from the potential promotion list so they could fill the position with a man of their choosing who had lesser credentials. In return for the favor, they would give Big Russ an even bigger salary bump. He turned them down, resulting in no raise or promotion for himself.

Big Russ told his son, "I know what I could have done with the money, but I also knew what that money would do to me…And how could I tell you kids to do the right thing if I ever did something like that?"

"That story means the world to me," wrote Tim Russert. "Dad didn't get the promotion, but he kept his honor."

The wise will inherit honor. (Psalm 3:35)

Lord, help me to choose integrity over personal gain.

Boston Strong

"Located across the street from Mass General Hospital in downtown Boston. I have a couch and an inflatable twin bed for anyone who needs a place to stay."

In the immediate aftermath of the Boston Marathon bombings on April 15, 2013, many messages like that were posted online by ordinary people wanting to help the victims' families by offering them a place to stay or some other assistance. And there were plenty of other examples of the terrorism bringing out the best in all Bostonians.

Marathoners who finished the race uninjured ran to the hospital so they could donate blood; former New England Patriots player Joe Andruzzi, whose cancer foundation supported the marathon, carried the injured out of harm's way; spectator and peace activist Carlos Arredondo saved the life of runner Jeff Bauman, whose legs were blown off, by applying pressure to his wounds to keep him from bleeding out.

Yes, darkness was on display that day. But so were many shining examples of light.

Whatever is honorable...think about these things. (Philippians 4:8-9)

May tragedy bring out the best in us, Prince of Peace.

You Are Free!

Rabbi Herschel Schacter became the first Jewish chaplain to enter the Nazi's Buchenwald concentration camp after General Patton's Third Army liberated it in 1945.

As reported in *The New York Times*, Rabbi Schacter drove through the camp's gates only to be met by the stench of burning flesh and the sight of dead bodies all around. He asked an American lieutenant, "Are there any Jews alive here?" The soldier took him to a barracks where "men lay on raw wooden planks stacked from floor to ceiling."

Rabbi Schacter exclaimed to them, "Peace be upon you, Jews, you are free!" He went to every barrack he could find proclaiming that same piece of good news. The *Times* writes, "He would remain at Buchenwald for months, tending to survivors, leading religious services…and eventually helping to resettle thousands of Jews."

Rabbi Schacter died in 2012 at age 95. Rabbi Yisrael Meir Lau, who was a boy in Buchenwald, remembered him as delivering survivors "from death to life."

Peace be to you; do not fear. (Judges 6:23)

Guide us toward peace and freedom, Heavenly Father.

Carrying Each Other's Crosses

The Bible often speaks of the importance of bearing one another's burdens. In doing so, our own burdens are subsequently lightened. It's no small wonder that Carolyn Woo, president and CEO of Catholic Relief Services, praises the example of Simon of Cyrene, a single man from the crowd who helped Jesus carry the cross on which He would be crucified.

"I identify with this station [of the Cross]," Woo wrote in *Catholic News Service,* "because Simon and his service happen over and over again in my experience. A good friend once asked whether I get depressed over the suffering that we see in our work. The answer is no. I feel deep concern and sadness over what people have to endure...but not hopelessness."

It is in suffering that people from all walks of life are brought together, united by a common determination and hope for a better tomorrow. "Like Simon, we do not intentionally go seeking the needy," Woo concludes, "but due to forces beyond our control, we may be 'compelled' to help carry a cross."

Bear one another's burdens, and in this way, you will fulfill the law of Christ. (Galatians 6:2)

Jesus, may we always be moved to help others.

Spitting in the Face of God

There is no scene more heartbreaking and simultaneously reflective of God's love for mankind than His Son's holy Passion. Meekly and uncomplainingly, Jesus endured scourging and whipping at the hands of Roman soldiers. He was also mockingly called the "King of the Jews" while being crowned with thorns. Most humiliating of all, however, Christ's face was repeatedly spit upon by these aforementioned merciless men.

"In relation to the whipping and scourging," *Catholic Times* writer Leandro M. Tapay says, "the soldiers were following orders, but the actions committed in between are hard to comprehend...Who other than Satan and his minions, acting through their human agents on earth, could have attained pleasure from spitting on a man who was already half-dead?"

According to Tapay, modern ways in which we "spit" on others and, by extension, on Christ are gossiping, arguing, bragging, etc. Only by adhering to Jesus' steadfastly selfless example can we keep from adding more negativity to the world.

Therefore be imitators of God, as beloved children, and live in love, as Christ loved us. (Ephesians 5:1-2)

God, may we keep our minds and hearts free from impurity.

Why Jesus Wept

In her Christopher Award-winning spiritual memoir *My Sisters the Saints,* author Colleen Carroll Campbell chronicles her father's slow descent into Alzheimer's disease. She also writes about the powerful lesson she learned about life, death and God in the moments after he died.

Campbell says, "I thought of that story in the Gospel where Jesus is told that His friend Lazarus has died. 'He wept,' it says, in a line that always puzzled me. Why would Jesus—the all-powerful, all-knowing Savior who conquered death by His resurrection—weep?

"Remembering how Dad's broken-down body had strained violently for every breath at the end, I finally understood. Jesus wept because death is a horror...even the death of someone on his way back to God. Jesus wept because death, like Alzheimer's...was never what He wanted for us. It was not part of God's original plan. Jesus saved us from death's finality; He brings greater good out of its pain; but death still horrifies us because that's the very nature of death: horrifying."

You have delivered my soul from death. (Psalm 56:13)

Comfort the grieving, Divine Redeemer.

A Broken and Beautiful World

"This world is as broken as it is beautiful," wrote singer-songwriter Brooke White on Twitter after the Sandy Hook Elementary School shootings, which left 20 children dead in December 2012. Evidence reflects the truth of those words.

Each of us is capable of beautiful acts of kindness, sacrifice and self-denial. For Christians, this world was saved by beauty. It was a beauty that started horrifically and paradoxically with a crucifixion, but ended with resurrection and hope and grace.

Despite that divine gift, however, we remain a broken people—a people who disrupted our lives in harmony with God a long time ago. We're all flawed and can hurt others as well as ourselves in either intentional or unintentional ways. We can make choices that take us further and further away from the life that God intended for us.

So in this broken, yet beautiful world, pray for all the hurting, troubled people. And remember to add your share of beauty to this life. God knows we need it more and more.

Do no wrong or violence to the alien, the orphan, and the widow, or shed innocent blood. (Jeremiah 22:3)

Teach us to aspire always toward kindness, Holy Spirit.

Resurrected Out of the Darkness

On Easter Sunday 2013, the people of Newtown, Connecticut, devastated by the school shootings at Sandy Hook a few months earlier, had every reason to doubt the goodness of God, even the existence of God. But according to a column by Denis Hamill in New York's *Daily News,* God's presence remained strong and, in some cases, had grown even stronger.

Jen Hubbard, for instance, had lost her daughter Catherine on that fateful December day. She told Hamill:

"I'm at complete peace, just as I was at total peace on Dec. 14 because I knew Catherine was with God. A lot of people have said, 'Oh, Jen's just avoiding it, in denial.' But I know full well what happened in that school. I choose not to dwell on that. To do that allows the Devil to win. God didn't do this. The Devil did, and he thought we would crumble. But the Devil was wrong. It has made us stronger physically and spiritually—as people, as families, as a town...Even though Catherine is missing in body, this will be a great Easter. Because out of the pain and out of the darkness, Newtown is resurrected."

[Jesus] has been raised. (Matthew 28:7)

Guide us toward a new life in heaven, Jesus.

A Healthy Grief

Raised Catholic in southern Louisiana, Jessica Mesman Griffith, co-author of the book *Love and Salt: A Spiritual Friendship Shared in Letters,* grew up surrounded by the overt religious practices native to the region. When her mother developed a terminal illness, her parents moved to an evangelical church in search of a healing miracle that never came.

Griffith grieved both the loss of her mother and her childhood faith. Yet the soulprints of Catholicism never left her, so she returned to the Church when she got older. One of the benefits was dealing with her mother's death in a spiritually healthy way for the first time.

During an interview on *Christopher Closeup,* Griffith said, "I needed to acknowledge death, to acknowledge that suffering was a reality....I needed to feel that this story was not over with my mother and the other people we had lost—that we were going to be able to have some connection with them. It's not something that's going to happen when we die. It's something that we have access to right now. There's not a wall between us and heaven. It's much more permeable than we might believe."

Death will be no more. (Revelation 21:4)

Heal my wounded heart and soul, Savior.

Granny the Pole-Vaulter

When some people hit age 65, they decide to retire and take it easy. Flo Meiler, on the other hand, took up pole-vaulting. It was actually just an extension of her track and field efforts, which she began at age 60 to take part in the Senior Olympics.

As reported by *CNN*, the now 79-year-old grandmother and great-grandmother from Shelburne, Vermont, holds 15 world records. They include the world indoor record in the pole vault for women over age 75, along with records in the discus, the hammer throw, and the 200-meter hurdles.

Meiler admits that some of her friends think she's "nuts" for keeping such an intense training and competitive schedule, but she loves to take on new challenges because they're rewarding. Her advice for seniors looking to try something new?

"If I can take up track and field at 60, anybody can take up another sport at age 50 and up...One of the recommendations I have been mentioning is go to their senior center...If they really want to...do something athletic, the center will have resources to help them find what they should do and how safe it can be."

Rich experience is the crown of the aged. (Sirach 25:6)

May I age with health and grace, Father.

An Approach to ADHD

"Although not all medical experts are in agreement about the degree to which sugary food impacts children's behavior...I've noticed that when my children have their cake and eat it, too, they're prone to becoming more reactive than plutonium."

So writes Kate Wicker in *Catholic Digest* about how sugar affects children's moods and behavior. Specifically, she's concerned about the amount of kids diagnosed with Attention Deficit Hyperactivity Disorder (ADHD), who are then given medication to control the problem.

Dr. Mary Ann Block, author of *No More ADHD*, has found that a simple diet change produces dramatic results. She says, "Sugar and artificial sweeteners are removed, and families feed the child only protein and water for breakfast. Not eating carbohydrates for breakfast seems to set the blood sugar for the rest of the day."

Wicker hasn't cut sugar out of her kids' diet completely. They eat wholesome snacks 80 percent of the time, and enjoy cookies the other 20 percent. In other words, moderation is key.

Overeating brings sickness. (Sirach 37:30)

Creator, help me make healthy and wise eating choices.

A New Serenity Prayer

Mike Hayes, the Director of Campus Ministry at Canisius College in Buffalo, New York, wrote a new version of the Serenity Prayer on his blog, Googling God. It says:

"Lord, grant me the patience to keep my mouth shut when I am annoyed, the Strength to not let anger get the best of me, and the Wisdom to seek peace always in all things. I know I can be mean to people, even those close to me. I know I can take my frustrations out on others. I can be short-tempered and have high expectations that nobody could approach satisfying.

"But as [Thomas] Merton says: I do believe the desire to please You does in fact please You. So walk with me and further cultivate that desire for peace: peace in the world, peace in my heart, peace above all. For peace is not merely the absence of violence. Rather it is what keeps our hearts open to love…"

"Help me to stay open-hearted when I would rather close the doors to my own heart. For Your bleeding heart offered all its blood for us and hoped to create more hearts to bleed and beat for others. May that desire…become my own today. Amen."

The Lord is peace. (Judges 6:24)

Lord, make me an instrument of Your peace.

An Autistic Girl Finds Her Voice

Carly Fleischmann's family held little hope that they would ever be able to connect with the 10-year-old due to her severe autism, inability to speak, and intellectual impairments. But one day while working with her devoted therapists, Carly astonished everyone by typing a message on a keyboard. They discovered that she had understood much more than they ever thought possible during her early years of life; she just hadn't been able to communicate.

The Christopher Award-winning book *Carly's Voice* shares the Fleischmanns' story with brutal but inspiring honesty. And though she still struggles with the symptoms of autism, Carly now attends a mainstream school where she takes gifted classes.

There is a lot about autism that we don't understand. If the disorder affects your family in some way, seek out a support system. Also, pray for the guidance, wisdom and strength to make the best of the situation.

May those who sow in tears reap with shouts of joy. (Psalm 126:5)

For parents and children who struggle with infirmities, Lord, bless them with Your peace.

We'll Be Back

Say this about the Sullivans: they like doing things together. So when it came time to build their homes, five Sullivan brothers followed the example of their parents and settled in or near Breezy Point, in the New York City Borough of Queens (two more brothers live outside the New York area).

When Hurricane Sandy struck the Northeast with savage force at the end of 2012, Breezy Point was among the hardest-hit communities—and, one by one, members of the Sullivan family had to flee for their lives. As Denis Hamill reported in the *Daily News,* all of them lost their homes for what would be months at a stretch, and their parents, Russ Sr. and Ursula, had to be evacuated to the mainland in the middle of the night.

But as Michael Sullivan explained: "None of us was hurt or lost. We're all still alive. Like everyone else down here, we're down but not out. We'll be back."

And that sound you heard might have been all the Sullivan brothers agreeing: "We'll be back!"

We are afflicted in every way, but not crushed. (2 Corinthians 4:8)

Father, in times of tragedy, help us to keep faith and hope alive.

The Ex-Con Priest

Donald Callaway's background hardly made him an ideal candidate for the priesthood. In fact, he might have been the least likely future priest you've ever met. That background included an arrest, a term in rehab, and what's generally referred to as the "high life." Then, at his lowest, he read a book about Mary, the mother of Jesus. Not only did it change his life, he compared it to being hit by a spiritual two-by-four.

"When I discovered the faith that impacted how I lived," he told *Our Sunday Visitor,* "I cleaned up my act and started behaving like a normal human being."

That was only the beginning. He joined the church formally, and soon began studies for the priesthood—with the Marians, because he liked their devotion to Mary.

Ordained in 2003 as Father Donald Callaway, MIC, he's now a vocations director and spends a lot of time talking to those in jails and rehab centers. "They feel they can open up to me," he explains. "They think, 'Wow! He understands!'"

Depart from evil, and do good. (Psalm 27:27)

Jesus, release us from the snares of our sins.

By the Toss of a Coin

Often, a coin toss may decide nothing more than who gets the ball first in a game. And yet, there are examples of history made on the call of "heads" or "tails"—even when it seemed the wrong call.

When Wilbur Wright made the correct call of the coin, he won the chance to have the first try at flying, beating brother Orville to that task. Ironically, it was Orville who eventually got the plane airborne.

Although Penny Chenery lost the coin toss to see who would get first pick of two foals sired by a prominent racehorse, she ended up the winner—getting a colt who would be named Secretariat and who would win horse racing's Triple Crown.

Life's decisions often need more thought than a simple coin call. But it's good to know that even a bad choice can be turned around.

Whatever you do, in word or deed, do everything in the name of the Lord Jesus, giving thanks to God the Father through Him.
(1 Colossians 3:17)

Bless me with Your wisdom, Master.

Sleeping on the Right Side of the Bed

How many of us complain of lack of sleep because we simply can't fall asleep? Maybe we're too tired, not tired, worried or wired. Here are some ideas to make sure you start the night's rest right:

- Give yourself a bedtime. *Happiness Project* author Gretchen Rubin says to look to the time you have to get up, and count backwards for the seven hours of sleep you need.

- Slow down. Sending e-mails and playing games on your Smartphone are not pre-bedtime activities. Rubin notes: "Let your mind wind down."

- Set a routine. Establishing certain tasks you do every night before bed becomes a calming ritual, Rubin explains.

Our hearts remain ever restless, content only as they find peace in knowing the Lord and trusting in His love.

I will grant peace in the land, and you shall lie down, and no one shall make you afraid. (Leviticus 26:6)

Lord, I am weary; give me rest.

Communicating Through Photography

Although families survived what became known as the government-sanctioned slaughter of the Killing Fields in Cambodia, physical, mental and emotional scars remain. According to the *Daily News,* the years 1973 to 1979 saw "the slaughter of two million Cambodians by the Khmer Rouge."

Pete Pin uses photography to explore the tormented experiences of his people. Born in a refugee camp before his family came to the U.S., he traveled across this country documenting the everyday lives of Cambodians in America. The result is his photo exhibit "Cambodian Diaspora."

"This work was an opportunity to connect with the past, starting with my own family history, then to the collective history of the Cambodian diaspora," says Pin. "I realized that I could explore the complexity of my identity and the experiences of my people through photography."

How can you use your talents to shed light on your own identity and your family's history?

The sun of righteousness shall rise, with healing in its wings. (Malachi 4:2)

Holy Spirit, inspire us to overcome barriers that separate us from others.

Don't Say It Can't Be Done

Richie Parker drives a car and engineers chassis and body components for NASCAR's Hendrick Motorsports, which boasts Dale Earnhardt Jr. and Jimmie Johnson as clients. That may not sound like a big deal until you realize that Parker has no arms.

After Parker was born in 1983, his parents tried to give him as normal an upbringing as possible, teaching him to use his chin, shoulders and feet to pick things up, open doors and even use a computer.

As the Buford, North Carolina native got older and grew determined to be more independent, he developed an interest in cars, especially the 1964 Chevy Impala SS. He bought the vehicle from its previous owners, and had it fitted with a special disc on the floor that he uses to steer.

When Parker started working for Hendrick, some co-workers wondered if he'd be able to do the job. Eight years and five NASCAR championships later, he's proven he can. As he told *ESPN*, "I don't know that there's a whole lot in life that I can say that I can't do—just things that I haven't done yet."

For God all things are possible. (Mark 10:27)

May I face all challenges with hope, Lord

The Cultural Antidote of Gratitude

Boston College High School theology teacher Patrick Tiernan, responding to an invitation from the Ignatian Educator website, offered these words of advice to graduating seniors:

"The world will entice you to live in an endless state of desire, but I invite you to indulge in the cultural antidote of gratitude. Being grateful leads to humility, which ultimately helps you to turn inward and discover the love that is at the core of all true relationships. This is difficult to experience at times because we live in an age of 'thin thoughts' with tweets and texts. By cheapening language, we risk underestimating the depth of genuine intimacy.

"Relationships are messy, complicated, and confusing intersections of the heart and head, spiritual investments that demand our whole being. Who we become reflects these relationships and those we allow to enter into our story, our incomplete narrative that, in many ways, writes itself. Be open to that feeling of suspense toward the mystery that is your future; it is fraught with angst and bliss but well worth the wait."

There is hope for your future. (Jeremiah 31:17)

Help us to ground our lives in gratitude, Father.

Hero Teachers

Shielding students with their own bodies, teachers at Plaza Towers and Briarwood Elementary Schools in Moore, Oklahoma, were heroes the day that tornadoes ripped through their small town in May of last year.

"I had them take their backpacks and put them over their heads as another safety precaution," said Sherry Brittle of Briarwood Elementary School. Her fellow teacher, Cindy Lowe, added, "[I lay] my body on top of as many kids as I could to help out."

At Plaza Towers, one rescue worker told the *Today Show,* "We had to pull a car out of the front hall off a teacher. I don't know what her name is, but she had three little kids underneath her." Miraculously, they all survived.

To preserve and protect life is the call the Lord sends to us all—in ordinary and extraordinary circumstances alike.

Turn, O Lord, save my life; deliver me for the sake of Your steadfast love. (Psalm 6:4)

Shelter me in life's storms, Master. Send me Your hope.

A Balloon of Hope

On the Sunday after Easter, in 2001, second-grader Abby Steger stood outdoors with the rest of her First Communion class in Edgewood, Iowa, and released a balloon with a poem and personalized message written inside of it. Little did Abby dream that 11 years later her balloon would be recovered by a married couple, Mark and Kathy Harwick, in Hatfield, Wisconsin.

"It was unbelievable," Steger told *Catholic News Service*. "I was in total shock. I never thought it would be returned."

"We've received some [notes] back with the balloon still attached," said Jody Kerns, director of religious education at St. Mark's in Edgewood. "Typically, the person who finds it will send a note or say something about how they found it."

The Harwicks dug Steger's note out of a culvert near a storm after a major flood. Harwick told Kerns that after her husband read the note, a rainbow appeared, and "it reassured him spiritually at a difficult time."

It just goes to show, as Steger said, "one little note can make a difference."

Set all your hope...on Jesus Christ.
(1 Peter 5:13)

Lord, may we always be inspired by everyday miracles.

Superwoman Needs Help

Sallie Felton admits that she used to consider herself a superhuman wife, mother and daughter who could accomplish everything by herself. Though she kept a smile on her face, inside she felt miserable. The reason? She needed help, but couldn't bring herself to ask for it.

Felton finally worked up the courage and conviction to ask her fellow family members for assistance. Yes, the kids whined about doing extra chores, but Felton stood her ground. Now, she advises others who feel overwhelmed to do the same.

Felton writes, "What's one area in your life you want extra help? Childcare, laundry, workload, chores, housework…the list could be endless. Here is the secret! You have a CHOICE! And it's all yours! You can choose to be stressed, overwhelmed, and ride the rollercoaster, or you can choose to ask. But you have to be willing to let go of expectation and perfection. Someone may not set the table, do the dishes, clean the house exactly as you wish, but here's the point: Is the Task Getting Done? YES, yes, yes it is!!! So take the risk and ask."

Ask, and it will be given you. (Matthew 7:7)

Break through my pride, Lord. Let me ask for help.

A Long Shot Pays Off

Brazilian bicyclist Leandro Martins has taken on the daunting task of cycling 6,200 miles from Amsterdam to Asia. But perhaps his most unlikely accomplishment came when Pope Francis agreed to meet with him for a while.

As reported by the *Huffington Post,* Martins isn't Catholic, but he admires the Pope's simplicity and commitment to the poor. He sent several letters to the Pope's secretary requesting a meeting. Martins wrote, "I know I am not an important person…but maybe I am also a sheep of God…and that makes me feel that if I believe from the bottom of my heart that it is possible, it really can happen."

Martins' persistence was rewarded on July 18, 2013, when he cycled into the Vatican for a brief visit with Pope Francis. They engaged in a friendly conversation about Brazil—and Martins' gave the Pope a picture drawn by the nephew of a nun he knew. Before parting ways, the two new friends took a picture together, and the Pope signed Martins' Brazilian flag with the words, "May God accompany you." Not a bad day for a humble cyclist who took a chance and saw it pay off.

He welcomed them. (Luke 9:11)

Help me be welcoming to strangers, Jesus.

Family, Faith and Blue Bloods

The CBS TV series *Blue Bloods* stars Tom Selleck, Donnie Wahlberg, Bridget Moynahan, Will Estes, and Len Cariou as members of the Reagan family who have each committed their lives to law enforcement in some way. Though crimes are solved in each episode, the show is ultimately a family drama that highlights love, loyalty and faith. For that reason, The Christophers honored *Blue Bloods* with our 2013 Special Christopher Award.

The Reagans pray and eat together every Sunday in order to keep the family bonds between them strong. Selleck has said that fans approach him to say the dinner scenes are their favorite because they reflect what family should be.

The Reagans' faith also plays an integral role in their lives, as something they both rely on and wrestle with because of the tragedies they witness. The walk of faith isn't easy, but Cariou's character may sum it up best—for the Reagans and for viewers—when he says, "I see God's light in this family every day. And though I may not understand it, I trust in His plan for us all."

Love the family of believers. (1 Peter 2:17)

Father, help all families stay united and strong.

Shared Values Over Bagels

A couple of Muslim cabbies rescued one of New York City's oldest Jewish bakeries from closure in 2011.

Peerzada Shah, who was attending a Manhattan culinary arts school in addition to driving a taxi, and Zafaryab Ali, a former baker on staff at the landmark Coney Island Bialys and Bagels, took over the store after it became clear that the business was about to shutter its doors. Ali wanted to keep it in the spirit of its original owner, Morris Rosenzweig, a Jewish immigrant from Poland.

One long-term employee was set to retire but planned to stay awhile and help the new owners adjust. "The two men are very, very good-natured, well-intentioned and just good people," he told *MSNBC*. "They want to keep the bakery kosher and I want to help them succeed."

Bridging differences to create unity is always a worthwhile endeavor. And if you throw bialys and bagels into the mix, so much the better!

Maintain the unity of the Spirit in the bond of peace. (Ephesians 4:3)

May we always remember our shared values, Dear God.

Caring for Caregivers

Taking care of ailing patients is a real challenge whether we're a family member, a friend or a health-care professional.

Retired hospital chaplain Patricia Normile knows this well and writes about it in *St. Anthony Messenger.* She notes, "Health-care issues are real: How do I stay healthy? Find proper care, pay the bills?"

While pragmatic concerns must be addressed, another essential element for health and wholeness is often overlooked: "That element is the spiritual well-being of those who care for the sick, the aged or the dying."

Some spiritual issues include the power of prayer, the need to care for oneself, dealing with guilt and resentment and the need for forgiveness. "Prayer strengthens caregivers for tasks they may not feel capable of performing," Normile writes.

Self-care isn't selfish; it's essential. One caregiver is restored by a daily bath. Others share their struggles with various church or social-support groups.

Remember, caregivers need care, too.

The Lord is my helper. (Hebrews 13:6)

Help us, Jesus, to support caregivers in their daily tasks.

No Remorse About Motherhood

Model and entrepreneur Summer Bellessa chose to spend more time at home after giving birth to her son, Rockwell. After seeing a segment on television about a mother who felt "remorse" for staying home with her kids, she reflected on the bad rap some women get for prioritizing family over career.

On her blog, The Girls with Glasses, Bellessa wrote, "You can't put a price tag on your time with your kids, no matter how much money you have lost in possible wages. Raising kind, smart and healthy children is the biggest impact anyone can ever have on the world."

The Phoenix, Arizona resident added, "If you stay at home, you still have the opportunity to help within the community, to develop other talents, and go outside your smaller circle. It might not be as easy as being thrown together with a bunch of coworkers, but it can sometimes be more meaningful too."

Finding the right balance between career and motherhood can be a challenge. Pray for the guidance and support to do what's best for you and your family.

Do not forsake your mother's teaching. (Proverbs 6:20)

Help me be there for my family, Lord.

A Christopher Prayer for Mother's Day

Lord, today we thank You for our mothers: the ones who gave us life, the ones who chose us through adoption, and the unofficial mothers who were a strong and compassionate presence when our biological mothers weren't up to the task.

We remember the love with which they cared for us when we were most vulnerable; the tears they dried and fears they soothed when we were troubled; the encouragement they offered when we had little faith in ourselves; the guidance they provided when we felt lost; the worries they endured when we were growing up; the strength it took to hold us close, yet let us fly.

We pray that our mothers who are no longer with us are embraced by Your love in the next life; that future mothers, expectant mothers and new mothers experience the joys that come from putting a child's needs ahead of their own, even when the sacrifices seem challenging; that our mothers who are still living experience Your enduring and ever-present love through the appreciation and gratitude that we, their children, show them not just this day, but throughout the year. Amen.

Honor your mother. (Tobit 4:3)

Bless and protect all mothers, Heavenly Father.

Righting a Wrong

Occasionally you'll hear about a robber guiltily returning stolen merchandise. But settling accounts 60 years after the fact?

A recent news report notes the experience of one elderly man who confessed to stealing from a Seattle department store decades ago. He paid the cash back with interest in a hand-delivered envelope. His note read:

"During the late forties I stole some money from the cash register in the amount of $20-$30. I want to pay you back this money in the amount of $100 to put in your theft account."

Customers found the gesture awesome and heartwarming. The store manager thinks the man's "conscience must have been bothering him for the past 60 years."

Although security cameras caught the man dropping off his envelope, store personnel said they didn't recognize him and weren't inclined to pursue the matter. They planned to contribute the money to a fund for needy families.

It is possible to make amends long after the fact.

If they repent with all their heart and soul... forgive Your people. (1 Kings 8:48-50)

God, help us atone when we're in the wrong.

Comforting Care

Medical writer Karen Rafinski notes that palliative care is often confused with hospice care, even by doctors.

Both forms of care focus on helping patients manage pain, for instance. They use an interdisciplinary team approach and offer various services such as counseling.

"But if hospice care is about a good death, palliative care is about making the most of life with a serious illness, whether the disease is terminal or not," writes Rafinski in the AARP bulletin.

Hospice helps people who no longer need or want to treat their disease. Patients with palliative care are still fighting their condition and studies show it makes a difference in quality of life. More information is available from sites like getpalliativecare.org or palliativedoctors.org.

"Patients should not be afraid to ask for a palliative care consultation," says researcher Thomas Smith, M.D. "It doesn't mean they'll die sooner. In fact, they might live better and longer."

This is my comfort in my distress, that Your promise gives me life. (Psalm 119:50)

Comfort us, Lord, during our times of need.

Dreams of Possibility

The Chief Rabbi of England's United Hebrew Congregations, Lord Jonathan Sacks, often gets asked for advice by college graduates moving into a new phase of their lives. The first thing he tells them is to dream.

Rabbi Sacks writes, "The least practical activity turns out to be the most practical, and most often left undone. I know people who spend months planning a holiday but very little time planning a life. Imagine setting out on a journey without deciding where you are going to...You will never reach your destination because you never decided where you want to be."

Rabbi Sacks concludes, "Dreams are where we visit many lands and landscapes of human possibility and discover the one where we feel at home. Within my own tradition there was Moses, who dreamed of a land flowing with milk and honey, and Isaiah who dreamed of a world at peace. One of the greatest speeches of the 20th century was Martin Luther King's 'I have a dream.' If I were to design a curriculum for happiness, dreaming would be a compulsory course."

He leads me in right paths. (Psalm 23:3)

Guide me to make the right choices, Holy Spirit.

The Egg Lady

She's known as "The Egg Lady," but her reach goes far beyond a carton of eggs. Lynn Goodman-Strauss earned that name because each morning at 7:30 she stands at a day labor corner in Austin, Texas, handing out hard-boiled eggs. That's just for starters. She also has coffee and tortillas for those who want them, and then she gets to the business at hand: running Mary House, the Catholic Worker residence in Austin.

There she's a whirlwind of activity, especially with the homeless. She drives some to AA meetings, lets others have free showers, and hands out clothes. She never forgets a prayer, either, assuring her clients that everything she gives away has an Ultimate Source.

In short, Lynn Goodman-Strauss reaches out a hand where others might recoil in fear. She lives the life of a Christopher every day, but has little time for compliments. Instead she'd prefer to boil some more eggs, then head back to the streets and start the routine all over again.

But when you give alms, do not let your right hand know what your left hand is doing...and your Father who sees in secret will reward you. (Matthew 6:3,4)

God, may we labor honestly in Your righteous name.

The Potato Chip's Beginnings

In the summer of 1853, in a resort in Saratoga Springs, New York, one diner sent back his French fries to the kitchen, complaining they were too thick. The chef, George Crum, mildly insulted, decided to go to the other extreme, sending out paper thin fries. They were a hit, and the "Saratoga Chip"—later called the potato chip—was born.

Soon after, Crum opened his own restaurant, putting baskets of his chips on every table. Before a new century dawned, Crum's chips would become an item for sale at grocery stores.

Today, the dish created as a response to criticism tops America's favorite snack list. In fact, one estimate puts U.S. annual retail sales of potato chips at more than $6 billion.

Sometimes our mistakes open our eyes to better possibilities—for us and those around us.

I am about to do a new thing; now it springs forth, do you not perceive it? I will make a way in the wilderness and rivers in the desert. (Isaiah 43:19)

Keep me open to the wonder around me, Creator; to all the gifts You have given me.

The Strength in Humility

From a worldly, self-centered perspective, the virtue of humility is seen as a rather lowborn quality, often portrayed as a false veneer for a deeper sense of excessive self-worth. Yet, according to Church teaching, the quality of being truly humble points Christians towards a more selfless, fulfilling way of living

"First, humility directs us outward, not inward," *Catholic News Service* reporter H. Richard McCord explains. "It is more about our relationships with others and with God and less an attitude about ourselves. Second, humility is an active virtue with behavioral consequences. It's not a retreat into passivity or inactivity...Humility gives us the strength to let God be God and to realize we are not God."

God exults not only in our repentance, but in our actions that give meaning to our humble spirits. May we always be genuinely modest in the eyes of our Lord.

Blessed are the meek, for they will inherit the earth. (Matthew 5:5)

Abba, may we value our successes without growing prideful.

Cycling for Charity

For 50-year-old motorcyclist John Mascari of Indianapolis, divine inspiration struck in Colorado's Rocky Mountains, at almost 15,000 feet above sea level.

"You know how God sometimes puts ideas in your head, and He won't leave you alone?" Mascari asked *Criterion* writer John Shaughnessy. "That's what God did with me that day. It was like a light bulb went off in my head. I must have been closer to God in the mountains so He reached down...and drove the idea right between my ears."

The Indiana native got the idea to form a Catholic motorcycle club that would bring together both people and bikers. Additionally, all of this organization's proceeds would go towards assisting archdiocesan charities, so it would be an exercise in generosity as well as physical activity.

"I just hope there are a lot of like-minded people who want to do good," John Mascari concludes about his upcoming first meeting at St. Lawrence Parish. "And we'll have fun, too."

The human mind plans the way, but the Lord directs the steps. (Proverbs 16:9)

Jesus, may we have faith in Your ability to work good through us.

Standing Up to Bullies

In the Christopher Award-winning biography *Fearless: The Undaunted Courage and Ultimate Sacrifice of Navy SEAL Team SIX Operator Adam Brown,* author Eric Blehm recounts the development of Brown's character growing up in Hot Springs, Arkansas during the 1970s and 80s.

Blehm explained on *Christopher Closeup,* "Adam's parents always said if you see somebody being bullied on the playground and you don't stand up for them, you're just as bad as the bully."

As a result, Brown developed a reputation for looking out for the underdog. One example involves a boy with Down Syndrome named Richie Holden. Blehm said, "Some kids were...blocking [Richie] on the way to class, making fun of him. Adam, at age 13, stood between them. These guys were a foot taller than Adam, but he said, 'If you want to pick on somebody, pick on me.' They backed down. Adam put his arm around Richie and walked him to class."

So how did a good kid like Brown become a criminal? More of the story tomorrow.

Do not avert your eye from the needy. (Sirach 4:5)

Give me the courage to stay true to my principles, Lord.

Finding God Through Tough Love

Though Adam Brown grew up as a model of courage and compassion, he changed when a group of college friends convinced him to try crack cocaine. He started stealing in order to buy more drugs, and wound up a criminal with 11 felonies.

Brown's parents, Larry and Janice, were devastated when they found out what was going on. Though they weren't churchgoers, they joined a local Baptist congregation and put Adam in God's hands. Spiritual support from the pastor and prayer community helped the Browns take a "tough love" approach with their son: they had him arrested.

That's when Adam's life began its turnaround because he found God in jail and started reading the Bible.

Adam eventually married a woman named Kelley, who stuck by him through his relapses into addiction because she was determined to bring out the positive qualities she knew existed inside him. It was Kelley who inspired him to set a new goal for his life: to join the Navy.

The conclusion of Adam's story tomorrow.

The Lord...saves the crushed in spirit. (Psalm 34:18)

Redeemer, help those struggling with drug abuse.

A Tender Warrior's Sacrifice

The depth of character and fortitude that Adam Brown had shown in his past convinced the Navy to give him a chance. In the military, he rediscovered the values that he had been missing since high school. Becoming the father of two children also helped him move beyond his drug-abusing, criminal past.

While serving in Afghanistan, Brown became a tender warrior who distributed shoes and socks that he'd collected to the native children because he saw they had frostbitten toes.

Tragically, Brown was killed in Afghanistan on March 17, 2010. He'd known the worst could happen, so when he prepared his "last request" letter to his family, he asked that his entire life be remembered—the good and bad—so he could inspire others to find faith and strength despite their troubles.

Eric Blehm, author of *Fearless,* the biography about Brown's life, said, "Adam could have been dead in a ditch 15 years ago. He overcame and touched many people's lives. It's a great example of how a story that's dark can become light, how somebody can inspire from the grave."

A good name lasts forever. (Sirach 41:13)

Lord of second chances, guide our way.

The Vulnerability of Love

Truly loving another person can seem like a dangerous proposition because it opens you to the possibility of getting hurt. Yet the alternative, as author and theologian C.S. Lewis points out in his book *The Four Loves*, is far worse.

Lewis wrote, "To love at all is to be vulnerable. Love anything and your heart will be wrung and possibly broken. If you want to make sure of keeping it intact you must give it to no one, not even an animal. Wrap it carefully round with hobbies and little luxuries; avoid all entanglements. Lock it up safe in the casket or coffin of your selfishness. But in that casket, safe, dark, motionless, airless, it will change. It will not be broken; it will become unbreakable, impenetrable, irredeemable. To love is to be vulnerable."

Don't let fear or shallow pursuits keep you from opening your heart to genuine, selfless love. Loving others is the surest way to move closer to God Himself, who is the ultimate source of all love.

If I have all faith, so as to remove mountains, but do not have love, I am nothing.
(1 Corinthians 13:2)

Help me to choose love courageously and wisely, Jesus.

A Chaplain's Legacy

Emil Kapaun might have been just another farm boy in Kansas, but from the beginning he stood out from the rest. He stood out for his sense of purpose, rare indeed for a youth his age. He stood out in 1940, when he was ordained a priest; again when he became a World War II chaplain; and yet again when he was recalled during the Korean War.

And yet the most memorable days of Father Kapaun's priesthood were still ahead. He became a legend for refusing to leave the wounded, even under fire; and the legend only grew once he was taken prisoner. In camp he tended tirelessly to his soldiers, and quietly took on the most loathsome tasks himself even as his fellow prisoners argued about them. Finally illness caught up with him, and he died still a captive—at the age of 35.

The men never stopped talking about him, though, and eventually all the talking bore results. In a White House ceremony last year President Obama awarded him the Congressional Medal of Honor, posthumously, saluting him as a hero. And in that way, Father Kapaun will stand out forever.

Precious in the sight of the Lord is the death of His faithful ones. (Psalm 116:15)

Christ, bless our nation's heroes who led by example.

Sharing Christ Effectively

Through a youth program he co-founded called Dirty Vagabond Ministries, Bob Lesnefsky (aka Christian rapper Righteous B) found an effective way to share Christ with others.

Describing the Steubenville, Ohio-based ministry's approach as "incarnational," they place missionaries in urban areas to live among the people.

Lesnefsky explained on *Christopher Closeup,* "We show up at a park and start grilling hot dogs and feeding people. The first time, we just get to know their name. Over weeks or years, it eventually builds relationships and develops into a friendship. It's much more effective for me to share Christ with someone who considers me their friend than someone who I knock on their door and try to give them a five-minute plug. There's an element of trust that happens before we even tell them about God. They begin to see we care for them outside of whether or not they ever come to the Church."

Loving people is the foundation of bringing them to God.

Beloved, let us love one another, because love is from God. (1 John 4:7)

Lord, make me a reflection of Your love for Your children.

Military Wives, Unsung Heroes

Jill Copeland had never witnessed a military homecoming, and was moved by what she saw. Accompanying her friend Kinsey, whose husband had been serving in the Middle East, she asked how she dealt with the separation.

Kinsey responded, "Saying goodbye to my new husband five days after our wedding was the hardest thing I'd ever done. Instead of packing for a honeymoon, we were packing fatigues and boots for a war overseas. Would I ever see him again?...Would his time at war change him? Despite all this, I am very proud to be an army wife."

Writing on the *Verily* magazine blog, Copeland says she gained new insight that day: "These women...do diapers, dishes, take out the trash, mow the lawn, give baths, cook dinners, and read bedtime stories, alone. At the end of the day these women lay in bed at night alone, begging God to protect their husbands. These women serve our country in a profound way, and while they don't have a national holiday in their honor, they should be appreciated, thanked and admired every day of the year."

Bear fruit with patient endurance. (Luke 8:15)

Bless all military families with strength and patience, Lord.

From the Civil War's Ashes

Memorial Day is one of America's favorite holidays, and many towns claim the honor of having the first Memorial Day—or "Decoration Day," as it used to be known. One thing appears to be quite clear: Memorial Day emerged from the ashes of the Civil War, when casualties from both North and South reached epic proportions.

With whatever locality the honor lies, the idea caught on. Clearly the suggestion was a popular one. In time those who died in subsequent wars were added to the list of men—and more and more, the women—who fell in battle and were paid tribute on this holiday.

And so Memorial Day goes on, its exact origin of less and less importance and the memories it inspires meaning more all the time. That's something to keep in mind in the midst of the parades you see, the picnics you hold, the speeches you're likely to hear. Too many of your fellow Americans gave their lives so that all of these things can take place. Remember them this day.

This day shall be a day of remembrance for you. (Exodus 12:14)

May the memories of the fallen be eternal.

A Way with Words

It's nice to have a way with words. It's even nicer when your writing is impossible to label, and they give you a Pulitzer Prize to boot. That was the case with William Raspberry, a political commentator who died a couple of years ago. He specialized in social issues, and his column—always unpredictable—appeared in 200 newspapers across the country.

A black man himself, Raspberry often vexed civil rights leaders—as he did when he chided them for thinking too much about racism, and failing to do enough about it.

His column was eclectic, but always directed toward a happier place. Here he is, for example, on modern song lyrics: "Because I know words matter, I wish my children would get back to innocent, hopeful lyrics. I wish their music was more about love and less graphically about intercourse. I wish their songs could be less angry...and more about building a better world."

His was a voice of optimistic moderation—and how we miss it. Thankfully, his legacy of words lives on.

A word fitly spoken is like apples of gold. (Proverbs 25:11)

Eternal Word, may we think carefully before we speak.

Rejoice Always

Inspired by his 75th birthday in 2006, Father John Catoir, the former Director of The Christophers, wrote the following reflection in his book *A Simple Guide to Happiness:*

"Even though I'm in the sunset of my life, I still look forward to many more years. While enjoying the moment, I know that one day I will die; we all will. I don't dread the thought of it. Jesus said, 'Do not be afraid,' and I take Him at His word. Except for my arthritic knees, I find life exhilarating, and I am especially grateful for the gift of faith. More importantly I am in love with joy. I sense God's presence in all the beauty of the world. I am surrounded by love.

"The pains of this world are passing, whereas the joys of the soul are ongoing. We reap what we sow. Those who choose to be joyful, even in the midst of setbacks, are in a better position to follow St. Paul, who said, 'Rejoice always!' That may be hard to do, but with God's grace, it's not impossible...Dear Lord, lead me to Your joy day by day."

Let all who take refuge in You rejoice; let them ever sing for joy. (Psalm 5:11)

Holy Spirit, help me to choose joy today.

Raising the Bar on Friendship

Jesus said that there is no greater proof of love than the willingness to lay down your life for a friend. Seven-year-old Dylan Siegel took this ideal to heart, making it his mission to save the life of his best friend, Jonah Pournazarian, also seven.

Jonah was diagnosed with a genetic and thus far incurable disease called Glycogen Storage Disease Type 1B. Determined to help his friend "feel better," Dylan wrote and illustrated a book called *Chocolate Bar,* whose title derives from an expression the two boys use to describe something amazing.

All revenues from this book will go towards finding a cure for Jonah's disease. To date, *Chocolate Bar* has garnered an amazing profit of $200,000. "To think that a seven-year-old boy could write a book that could raise more money than all the medical foundations combined!" Professor Dr. David Weinstein, director of the Glycogen Storage Disease Program at the University of Florida told *NBC News.*

Dylan's shining example just goes to show that you are never too young or old to make a difference.

A friend loves at all times. (Proverbs 17:17)

Lord, move us towards selfless acts of friendship.

All About the Train Ride

Many commute by train to work. The travel option is often a matter of necessity, and not choice. But there are train travel opportunities that offer luxury—and luxurious views.

Consider the Royal Canadian Pacific. Ten restored 1920s railcars, which feature walnut paneling and sterling-silver place settings, make their way from Calgary on a seven-day Royal Canadian Rockies experience.

There's also the trip through Andalusia in Spain on the Al Andalus. On board, there's live music offered in a lounge car. Or perhaps a safari is more your speed—and the Rovos African rail fleet has what you need. One 15-day voyage takes travelers from Tanzania to Botswana to Zimbabwe to Zambia, allowing for game spotting along the way.

In our own life's journey, our choices should always reflect the best for ourselves—and our neighbors.

I do hope to see you on my journey and to be sent on by you, once I have enjoyed your company for a little while. (Romans 15:24)

Grant me Your wisdom, Lord, that I may choose wisely this day.

One Proud Batdog

Most baseball teams have a batboy or batgirl, who retrieves bats and loose balls. And then there's...batdog? That's right; batdog. The Thunder, the New York Yankees' double-A affiliate in Trenton, New Jersey, proudly had a batdog—Chase, a Golden Retriever, who spent more than a decade serving players and entertaining fans before his death last year at age 13.

"He was a good dog," said Yankee second baseman Robinson Cano, who came up through Trenton. "He was always good with the bat. He never left teeth marks." Added pitcher Joba Chamberlain: "It was cool to see all the things he did. Just the smile that he put on the kids' faces was so special."

Thunder GM Will Smith said: "His presence was the epitome of the wholesome family entertainment for which we strive."

The Thunder quickly found a replacement for Chase—his son, Derby, who began helping "Dad" a couple of years ago. So at Trenton, it's still "Play ball!" And the batdog legacy lives on.

Who teaches us more than the animals of the earth? (Job 35:11)

Christ, bless all animals, who bring joy into our lives.

The Hardest Choice

By the time the Nazis took over Vienna, Jewish doctor Viktor Frankl was already an authority on helping patients fight depression by finding meaning in their lives. The chief of neurology at Rothschild Hospital, he was given a visa to travel to the United States, where he could escape the round-up of Jews by Hitler's forces.

Dr. Frankl was faced with a dilemma, however. The Nazis were taking the elderly first, meaning his parents would soon become prisoners. Feeling responsible for their care, he sought an answer from God by visiting St. Stephen's Cathedral and wondering if he should leave his parents to their fate.

Upon returning home, Dr. Frankl saw a piece of rubble that his father had found. It came from a synagogue the Nazis had demolished, and partially included the words from the Commandment, "Honor your father and mother." Dr. Frankl took this as his sign to remain in Vienna. Though his parents and wife eventually died in the concentration camp, he helped many others survive by pointing them to their unique purpose in life.

The Lord will not forsake His people.
(Psalm 94:14)

Lord, guide me to make the right choice, which isn't always the easy choice.

A Rescuer Saves a Life

When a fire began inside the bedroom of eight-year-old Cody Ma, he ran into another room and shut the door. The fire soon spread through the Gresham, Oregon house, causing everyone else inside to evacuate.

Cody's father Alex tried to get upstairs to rescue the boy, but was unsuccessful because the house was engulfed in flames. When neighbors Eduardo Ugarte and his son Marcos arrived to help, they saw soot coming out of Alex's nose and mouth.

According to *KATU-TV,* Marcos quickly sprung into action. Marcos said, "I [grabbed a] ladder, and I propped it up on the window, and I crawled up the window and punched the screen out...and grabbed the boy and carried him down the ladder."

Cody's life was saved thanks to his quick-thinking neighbors. Alex said, "They're my son's heroes forever."

Be strong and courageous; do not be frightened or dismayed, for the Lord your God is with you wherever you go. (Joshua 1:9)

Grant us the wisdom and courage to help others in dangerous situations, Lord.

The Bride Gives Up Bridal Magazines

Most women start reading bridal magazines after they get engaged. Ironically, that's the point when Tess Civantos stopped reading them.

She realized that some of the suggestions these magazines make are ridiculous (example: personalized, monogrammed pillows for the seats of all the guests at the reception), while others operated under the assumption that having your family involved in wedding planning is an unrealistic burden.

Writing in *Verily* magazine, Civantos says, "In their attempt to defend the bride's self-expression and individuality, magazines may actually be engendering a culture of egotism and entitlement—and thus disappointment....As someone getting married, I submit that weddings are about much more than just us brides. They're about more than just the bride and groom, even. Weddings are about a promise and a new beginning, a commitment to caring about someone other than yourself. Weddings are about two families coming together and a new family forming."

Come to the wedding banquet. (Matthew 22:4)

Holy Spirit, give engaged couples the right priorities.

The Power of Deduction

Sherlock Holmes and Dr. Watson went camping. They pitched their tent under the stars and went to sleep. Sometime in the middle of the night, Holmes woke his companion up and said, "Watson, look up at the sky, and tell me what you see."

Watson replied, "I see millions and millions of stars."

Holmes asked, "And what do you deduce from that?"

Watson replied, "Well, it means that space is vast and full of planets, stars, galaxies and many, many mysteries that human life hasn't yet discovered. Theologically, it suggests that there is a powerful, intelligent God who created it all with some purpose in mind. What do you deduce from it, Holmes?"

Holmes replied, "Watson, you fool, it means that somebody stole our tent!"

It's great to see life's big picture, but don't overlook the little details that surround you each day.

**The Lord opens the eyes of the blind.
(Psalm 146:8)**

Clear my vision that I may always find You, Lord.

The Lazarus Project

Nathaniel Hawthorne's novel, *The Scarlet Letter*, written in 1850, continues to resonate with readers today because it timelessly portrays the struggle of a former sinner seeking redemption.

"This scenario is being played out over and over again across this country," Father Stephen Powley writes in *The Orthodox Observer*. "[Orthodox] men and women are coming out of prison, wanting to succeed in life, only to find rejection."

Just as Jesus called upon the crowd to "unbind" the newly resurrected Lazarus after he emerged from his tomb, so must we as Christians help release these prisoners from the weight of their past sins. One such Orthodox organization, fittingly named The Lazarus Project, has already aided notably in this cause.

The Lazarus Project is a year-long holistic program in which each participant is matched with two or three mentors, whose goal it is to help the former criminal assimilate into society. Thus far, this program has succeeded in leading prisoners to new lives.

The oppressed shall speedily be released; they shall not die and go down into the Pit. (Isaiah 51:14)

Abba, may we forgive others as readily as You forgive us.

A D-Day Hero's Prayer

It was 70 years ago today—June 6, 1944—that would be forever remembered as D-Day. Sadly, the number of Americans who know about D-Day and its significance drops a bit each year, but those who lived through it will never forget. The Allied invasion of France that hellish day succeeded at a brutal cost, but it would pave the way for the eventual end of World War II.

There were many American heroes on D-Day. One of them was Joseph Vaghi Jr. of Bethesda, Maryland, who died at 92 a couple of years ago. A beachmaster, he guided other troops ashore through mine fields, mortar blasts and machine-gun fire. A eulogist recalled that Vaghi had his men kneel down in their small boat and pray the *Our Father* before they landed. At his death he still treasured the map he held that day on Omaha Beach—and prayed daily for the 23 men from his unit who lost their lives in the invasion.

Joseph Vaghi didn't like the "hero" label, and he thought "the greatest generation" was used a bit too much. But both tags were more than appropriate. In fact, they fit him like a glove.

The prayer of the righteous is powerful. (James 5:16)

Messiah, may faith be our loyal companion until death.

No Need for a Younger Guy

Don't tell Ben Jones he's too old for what he does. From his post in Shelter Island, New York, he's on call around the clock, has been working on ambulance duty since the days of World War II, and may be the oldest active paramedic in the country. And, oh yes—he was 90 when Corey Kilgannon wrote about him last summer in *The New York Times.*

Jones shows no signs of slowing down, which is good news for the people on Shelter Island. The community, located off Long Island, has no emergency medical center, so it relies on Jones and his squad of 10 EMTs. As the group's only paramedic, which requires advanced training, it's up to Jones to get a patient who needs hospital care to the ferry, and then to the mainland.

At times a patient will balk when he gets a look at Jones and asks, "Can't you have one of the younger guys do this?" Jones is ready for that, usually with a quip. "Listen," he says, "I was around when they invented the I.V., so relax!"

Don't let age keep you from living your purpose.

The glory of youths is their strength, but the beauty of the aged is their gray hair. (Proverbs 20:29)

Lord, may we rejoice in life's blessings, no matter our age.

A Necessary Storm

The intense heat and humidity indicated to Patheos.com blogger Margaret Rose Realy that there was a storm on the way. Thankfully, it wasn't a dangerous storm, but rather one that brought a refreshing rain. It even inspired her to write a prayer:

"Dear Lord, I thank You for the storms that move through life. Though there is darkness, there is assurance of its passing. You send the rain to cleanse, the thunder to make us attentive, and the wind to remind us that all things move according to Your plan.

"Although I do not like the darkness, I know Your storms draw me down and away from the often consuming blaze of this world. And for every storm that moves across my heart, I will embrace it as a time to patiently wait for Your return.

"I pray to be strong enough to hold fast when storms become intense. And if I grow weary, to know I am not alone and to call out to angels, saints, and friends to shore me up. I praise You Lord for dark nights and stormy days that deepen my desire for You. Amen."

**He commanded...the stormy wind.
(Psalm 107:25)**

Father, guide us through the storms of life.

A Baseball Star Larger Than Life

What's a statue of a baseball star who was a standout for the Pittsburgh Pirates doing in New York?

Simple. The player is Roberto Clemente, arguably Puerto Rico's greatest contribution to Major League Baseball, and New York is the center of Puerto Rican culture in the U.S. Beside that, there's been no one like Clemente to appeal to Puerto Rican pride. He broke not only baseball records but racial barriers. Therefore, there's a statue of Roberto Clemente in New York—in Roberto Clemente State Park, no less. But it wasn't easy.

The city had long wondered why there was no statue of a prominent Puerto Rican within its boundaries, and more recently the focus zoomed in on commemorating Clemente, who was killed in 1972 during a mercy mission flight. The money needed seemed an insurmountable obstacle until a group of angels promised the funds—and provided them too.

Clemente's statue was dedicated last summer. In the words of David Gonzalez, in *The New York Times*, the statue—like everything else about the star—is slightly larger than life.

The flower falls...the word of the Lord endures. (1 Peter 2:24)

Paraclete, may we pursue heavenly glory.

How To Complain Successfully

Since life doesn't always proceed according to plan, especially when you're traveling, it pays to learn the art of complaining without coming across as too angry.

Writing in *AARP* magazine, Peter Greenberg outlines several strategies travelers can use to get positive results when problems arise.

- Talk to the on-site boss. "Why argue with a gate agent who has no power to change your ticket or a front-desk clerk who can't remove a charge? Keep your cool and insist on speaking to a manager or supervisor."

- Be realistic. You won't get the world, but you might get a food voucher or a discount to compensate for a bad experience.

- "If you don't get results on site, follow up in writing." Contact department directors with specific facts and documentation. If possible, join with other similarly aggrieved customers.

Complaining can be uncomfortable, but your efforts might fix a problem and improve the experience for others.

Draw near to the Lord, for He has heard your complaining. (Exodus 16:9)

Encourage us, Jesus, to fight the good fight.

Take Care of the Minutes

"Do not squander time for that is the stuff that life is made of," Benjamin Franklin warned over 200 years ago.

Most of us are likely to be somewhat casual about the value of time. It's hard for us to realize that we get only one chance at life. Unlike shooting a movie, there are no re-takes.

Parents and teachers would add great meaning and purpose to the lives of young people if they helped them learn to use time instead of kill time.

In 1749, the British statesman Lord Chesterfield wrote to his son, "Know the value of time; snatch, seize and enjoy every moment of it. No idleness, no laziness, no procrastination." And in another letter he advised, "Take care of the minutes, for the hours will take care of themselves."

Keep constantly in mind that "now" is the only time you can count on to fulfill the important role in life which God has assigned to you.

See, now is the acceptable time; see, now is the day of salvation! (2 Corinthians 6:2)

Keep me ever conscious, Lord, of the value of time.

Making Your Daughter Squirm

"Sometimes love means you need to make someone squirm." *Verily* magazine's Monica Gabriel learned that lesson from her father, who raised eight kids and wasn't bothered by his parenting style often making them uncomfortable.

She remembers her dad greeting her every morning with a big bear hug during her "angsty, grouchy" teenage years; telling her how beautiful she was when she felt insecure about her appearance; and joining her mother for the "sex talk" that many fathers would be happy to avoid.

Since research indicates that the quality of a woman's relationship with her father influences her social and romantic relationships with men, that discomfort served a purpose. Gabriel writes, "My Dad's bear hugs became an important assurance that this day—no matter how crummy—would turn out okay...And I began to have the clarity to look back on that sex talk …and see that my Dad did it because he loved me. My Dad was not going to let a little thing like discomfort stand between me and happiness, between me and love."

I will be your father. (2 Corinthians 6:18)

Strengthen the bonds between fathers and daughters, Lord.

Grace, Gold and Glory

One of the most impressive things about Olympic gymnast Gabrielle Douglas's memoir *Grace, Gold and Glory* is that even though it's her life story, she doesn't make it all about herself. The teen readily acknowledges that if it weren't for the sacrifices made by her mother, brother, and sisters, she would never have won two gold medals at the 2012 London Olympics.

Douglas's Christian faith also plays a key role in her success. During an interview on *Christopher Closeup,* she said, "My mom has always taught me and my siblings the Word, and I don't know what I would do without my strong beliefs. When I got hurt, I would meditate, 'By His stripes, I am healed.' And when I was having struggles in the gym, I kept quoting, 'I can do all things through Christ who strengthens me.'...I was recently watching my gymnastics competition [on video] and I saw my lips moving. That's me praying, something I do every competition and every time I'm about to go out there and compete."

Follow Gabrielle Douglas's winning ways by making prayer a regular part of your life.

Pray always. (Luke 18:1)

I place all my trust and hope in You, Lord.

Being a Better Dad

Let's hear it for all the dads out there! Last year at this time *Our Sunday Visitor* offered some tips that fathers should keep in mind—not to become perfect simply by following them, but helpful steps that will aid anyone who wants to be a better parent.

- **Make time for your kids.** Your children know your time is valuable; taking a few hours to be with them will let them know how loved they are.

- **Be a loving husband.** A strong marriage leaves an equally strong impression on children.

- **Don't fear intimacy.** It might not go with being macho, but it will help you become a better leader.

- **Let your kids see you make mistakes.** Children can learn a lot if they know their dads aren't perfect.

- **Ask for help.** Seeking everyone's input shows both strong leadership and a sense of humility.

> **For a father's blessing strengthens the houses of the children. (Sirach 3:9)**

> *Abba, may all fathers look to You as the epitome of parenthood.*

A Christopher Prayer for Father's Day

Heavenly Father, we ask You to bless our earthly fathers for the many times they reflected the love, strength, wisdom and mercy that You exemplify in Your relationship with us.

We honor our fathers for putting our needs above their own convenience and comfort; for teaching us to show courage and determination in the face of adversity; for modeling the qualities that would turn us into responsible, principled, caring adults.

Not all our fathers lived up to these ideals. Give them the grace to acknowledge and learn from their mistakes. Give us the grace to extend to them the forgiveness that You offer us all.

Help new and future fathers raise children grounded in a love for God and other people. Remind these fathers that treating their wives with dignity, compassion and respect is one of the greatest gifts they can give their children.

We pray that our fathers who have passed into the next life have been welcomed into Your loving embrace, and that our family will one day be reunited in Your heavenly kingdom. Amen.

Listen, children, to a father's instruction. (Proverbs 4:1)

Bless all fathers, Creator.

Push Across America

Ryan Chalmers' 3,300-mile trip began in Los Angeles and ended in New York. Only he didn't make the journey on a plane or train; he completed it in his wheelchair.

Born with spina bifida and unable to fully use his legs, the 24-year-old wheelchair racer and Paralympian agreed to "Push Across America," as his campaign was called, to raise awareness about what people with disabilities can accomplish. It took 71 grueling days in which Chalmers endured 13 flat tires and severe muscle pain from pushing his body beyond its usual limits. Yet, as he told Yahoo Sports when he arrived in New York City on June 16, 2013, "You see a little kid at the finish line who's just smiling at you...it makes the injury and pain go away. For me, that's what helped me push through."

A film crew documented Chalmers' trek and he plans to speak about it around the country. His message: "This isn't supposed to be easy. Not something of this magnitude...But you just have to embrace the difficult moments and enjoy the really fun times as well."

Suffering produces endurance. (Romans 5:3)

Give my body and spirit resilience, Divine Master.

'Little Hands, Big Hearts'

"Mom, they need our help," five-year-old Iowa native Connor Andres told his mother after seeing the destruction wreaked by Hurricane Sandy along the East Coast.

Touched by her son's desire to help others, Terri Andres contacted Shelley Tegels, the director of his preschool, Our Lady's Little Learners. Together, the two women established the Little Hands, Big Hearts foundation, which collected money from the preschool. Their efforts amounted to a check totaling $4,636, which was sent to hard-hit Resurrection School and parish in Jersey City.

Natural disasters, though devastating, bring out the best in people, especially children. Sister Eleanor Uhl, principal of Resurrection School, told *The Catholic Advocate* that "her students are still talking about what took place in Iowa...It touched their hearts. It made those who took part realize how blessed they are."

In times of tragedy, what matters the most is to know that people care, that you are not alone.

Defend the rights of the poor. (Proverbs 31:9)

Abba, bless our children, our generous models of faith.

Finding Happiness

Nancy Perry Graham, editor-in-chief of *AARP* magazine, felt "grumpy" because of pressures at work and home. She decided to ask three of her favorite "fun folks" what makes them feel happy and content.

News director John Curran, 59, recently diagnosed with a terminal illness, felt grateful for his loving wife and family as well as his faith. He says he has "an abiding feeling of optimism that my being does not end when the heart finally stops."

Dianne Belli, 60, is passionate about healthy aging and works with Asian-American elders. She says, "I have the experience to know that life goes on in the face of extreme challenges." Additionally, she and her husband try new things such as "dancing the Argentine tango!"

Bonnie Perry, 70, says the happiest time of her life started in her 40s. She got a master's degree, became a librarian and found work at her grandkids' school.

Don't let age keep you from loving, learning, and growing.

Let the wise also hear and gain in learning, and the discerning acquire skill. (Proverbs 1:5)

Open our eyes, Father, so we appreciate sources of joy

Suffering with Another

When you or someone you love is suffering, it can feel like you're in a boat, being tossed and turned by the raucous waves. It's hard to handle the powerless feelings and emotions that arise. Praying seems one-sided: Where are you, God?

It is in these times that we must visit the Lord in adoration, and see Him on the crucifix. Jesus knows firsthand what it means to suffer: thrown out of towns, rejected by friends, falsely accused and not defended in the face of lies, scourged and tortured.

Jesus carried His heavy cross up to Calvary, where He was nailed to it, and still offered up His own suffering for the sake of the whole world's sins. He was fully human and fully divine, sinless and blameless, and His free will decision to put Himself through such suffering for our sake is of much consequence.

You are never alone in your suffering—I am here, and I know your pain, says the Lord. Jesus helps transform pain into a love-generating catalyst so that we all may be reunited with Him in Paradise.

Share in suffering like a good soldier of Christ Jesus. (2 Timothy 2:3)

Lord, sanctify my soul and be with us in our pain.

A Bride-To-Be and a Drowning Child

It was a hot June day when Becki Salmon and Matt Werner posed for their engagement photos on the shore of Wissahickon Creek near Philadelphia, Pennsylvania. The creek is a popular place to cool off, so two kids were playing in the water nearby.

Suddenly, a friend of Salmon and Werner's who was with them noticed that the five-year-old boy who had been visible in the water could no longer be seen. Salmon, a paramedic and lifeguard, told *ABC News,* "I turned to look [and saw] his little head bobbing under the water. According to my friend and photographer, I pushed my fiancé out of the way and ran."

Concerned that the creek's undercurrents would suck the boy beneath the murky-looking water and carry him away, she quickly dove in, followed by the boy's mother. Salmon pulled him to shore and along with Werner, an EMT, and photographer Ken Beerger, a paramedic, cleared his lungs of water. What had started as a day to commemorate a couple's future life together became one in which they gave a child a second chance at his own future.

Be strong and courageous. (Joshua 1:6)

Guide my steps when others are in danger, Savior.

Does This Make Me Look Fat?

Girls and young women often compare their bodies to those of the celebrities and models they see in magazines. As a result, many feel ugly and even come to doubt their self-worth.

Author Mary DeTurris Poust realized this problem when her 10-year-old daughter put on a coat and asked, "Does this make me look fat?" It was especially shocking because the girl only weighed about 60 pounds at the time.

DeTurris Poust told her daughter that all those glamorous, thin women she sees in magazines tend to be airbrushed to make them look more perfect than they really are. Then, DeTurris Poust's husband reminded her of another possible problem.

During an interview on *Christopher Closeup*, she said, "My husband reminded me [that] if she hears me saying 'I don't like the way I look in something' or 'do I look fat in this,' that's going to be really powerful. Sometimes I forget that. Magazines are bad, but mothers also have to be careful of the messages we're giving our daughters by the way we live."

Do not judge by appearances. (John 7:24)

Help us to recognize and appreciate our inherent dignity as Your children, Father.

Art's Healing Power

The Zaatari refugee camp in Jordan is filled with 120,000 refugees from Syria's civil war, many of them children who are haunted by the extreme violence and death they've witnessed.

Enter Samantha Robison, a Washington, D.C.-area artist who travels to war-torn parts of the world on behalf of an organization she founded called AptART. As stated on the group's website, they "empower marginalized children to express themselves through art, as well as build awareness and promote prevention of issues affecting their lives."

Robison told the *Associated Press*, "There's a lot of violent tendencies and negative energy [here], so if you bring in art and give [kids] a positive activity, it helps a lot."

Children paint pictures and murals on walls using bright colors to raise spirits. Says 12-year-old Habeer, "I am happy when I am painting...I want to be a teacher."

That happiness can be a vital resource in building a better tomorrow for these young people who've lost everything. It's also a tribute to the power of art and artists.

**The eye desires grace and beauty.
(Sirach 40:22)**

Creator, help us to inspire others through works of beauty.

What's That Summer Vacation About?

Summer vacation started because of work—farm work, in fact. In early U.S. history, schools educated mostly the children of farmers. And so the school year had to end in time to have those young people free to help their families on the farm, roughly May to October.

And while that may be true, the real reason the students' summer break stayed around—long after most U.S. families were farming—was to standardize school schedules across the country. If all students had more or less the same schedules, testing and textbooks could be more easily administered and utilized.

Whether still in school or long ago graduated, each of us needs to schedule down time—time off from our labors to nurture our relationships with others and to deepen our relationship with the Lord.

So God blessed the seventh day and hallowed it, because on it God rested from all the work that He had done in creation. (Genesis 2:3)

I find my peace in You, Father; slow me down.

An Inner City's Home Run

In October 2009, Washington, D.C. police officer Jason Medina heard gunshots while on patrol in Ward 7 near the Clay Terrace housing projects. When he arrived at the scene, he drew his weapon on the shooter: a 15-year-old boy, who surrendered.

That incident brought Medina back to his own troubled youth in Harlem, New York, where a program called Harlem RBI (Reviving Baseball in Inner Cities) provided him with the confidence, work ethic, and opportunity to build a better future. It's time to bring youth baseball to Ward 7, Medina thought.

He recruited coaches and mentors, and cleaned up a local field filled with beer bottles and hypodermic needles. Local youth became intrigued by the possibility of playing baseball.

Ward 7 Baseball has no budget other than what Medina and the coaches contribute out of their own pockets. But they're happy to be keeping kids out of trouble. As Medina told the *Washington Post,* "Even if 10 years from now we're still on a nothing budget, we'll still be here, as long as we can keep paying it forward."

Love one another as I have loved you.
(John 15:12)

Help me pay forward old kindnesses, Jesus.

Say Y.E.S. to Helping Others!

In June 2013, Fulton Street was teeming with Y.E.S. (Youth Encounter Service) volunteers rolling up their sleeves and working to improve this three-block area of Saginaw, Michigan. Their collective labor was focused on repairing three houses, their voluntary duties ranging from painting rooms to reconstructing wiring or plumbing. Whether first-time participants or seasoned veterans, volunteers are always happy they opted to say "Y.E.S."

"I have definitely learned to be more grateful for what I have," said high school student Erin Dwan of Blessed Trinity Parish to *Catholic Weekly's* Mark Haney. There is more to Y.E.S. than physical labor, though.

"Each year, young people are shown how difficult it can be just to get something to eat in a lower-income neighborhood," adds Mark Graveline, youth ministry director for the Diocese of Saginaw. "Ultimately, we want these young people to experience and to practice Catholic social teaching, which involves reaching out to the less fortunate as an act of love."

Give to everyone who begs from you. (Matthew 5:42)

Messiah, keep our minds and hearts open to those in need.

Welcome Back

There were *"alohas"* a-plenty last year for Father Stephen Macedo, who returned to active ministry in the Diocese of Honolulu, Hawaii, after an absence of 10 years. The sentiment shared by his bishop, his fellow priests and his parishioners was unanimous: "Nice to have you back!"

As reported in the *Hawaii Catholic Herald*, Father Macedo, 51, was ordained for the Hawaii diocese in 1993 and served in several parishes before leaving the active ministry 10 years later. He had lost to transfers the fellow priests who had been his friends and support group, and was feeling "pretty demoralized" over the clergy sex abuse scandal.

A full-time firefighter-EMT during his absence, he never stopped going to Sunday Mass and never married. He enjoyed the work but felt something was missing: "I missed preaching, being part of sharing the Good News. I missed celebrating the Eucharist and sacraments. I missed most of all being part of a parish community."

Father Macedo never lost touch with his faith. And he was welcomed back last year, with open arms.

Let us return to the Lord...He will heal us. (Hosea 6:1)

Christ, may we always return to Your loving embrace.

Your Guarantee of Heaven

Author Dan Lord used to see joy as a feeling you experience when doing something pleasurable. But through a lot of trial, error and soul-searching, he's come to see joy as a choice.

During an interview on *Christopher Closeup* about his book *Choosing Joy: The Secret to Living a Fully Christian Life*, Lord explained that an adult re-conversion experience to the Catholic faith of his childhood taught him that joy can be found through building a relationship with Jesus and following His whole "seamless garment of commandments" with an open heart. That's how even grumpy people, which Lord admits to being sometimes, can find joy despite their natural dispositions.

Lord explains, "Giving ourselves to the people God puts into our lives actually frees you...But the salvation that Jesus gives us isn't just a golden ticket to heaven like Willy Wonka. He's handing you a responsibility. He's saying, 'This is your guarantee of heaven if you choose it every day.' That's the responsibility that we have. But in doing that, joy blossoms."

Shout for joy, all you upright in heart.
(Psalm 32:11)

Help me reflect the joy of loving You, Father.

Friends — Your Lifesavers

There are certain things we know to do to stay healthy — exercise, eat more fruits and vegetables. And there are the things we know to avoid — smoking, stress.

But one cardiologist suggests that when it comes to overall health, your friends can save the day. "Friendship is a powerful healing force," says Dr. Joel Kahn.

Studies have shown, in fact, that peer support is a positive force in making healthy lifestyle changes.

Says Dr. Kahn: "There is an African proverb that states, 'If you walk fast, walk alone. If you want to walk far, walk together.' Grabbing someone's hand and walking together through challenges may be the most powerful health tool."

So what are you waiting for? Find a friend and start walking!

I take pleasure in three things, and they are beautiful in the sight of God and of mortals: agreement among brothers and sisters, friendship among neighbors, and a wife and a husband who live in harmony. (Sirach 25:1)

In all times, I count on Your abiding love, Master.

Peace Begins With You

Here is a bit of ancient Chinese wisdom that's worth a little reflection: "If there is righteousness in the heart, there will be beauty in the character; if there is beauty in the character, there will be harmony in the home; if there is harmony in the home, there will be order in the nation; when there is order in the nation, there will be peace in the world."

It's difficult to realize that peace in the world actually begins with each of us. Yes, it is within the power of one individual to do something, however slight, to make the world a trifle better. God Himself planned it this way. He assigned a special role for every human being to play as His instrument in supplying the goodness, truth and beauty which He intended for mankind.

Each of us can be a Christopher or Christ-bearer, and actually be a co-partner with God in helping not only our own little corner, but the entire world.

Peace I leave with you; My peace I give to you. (John 14:27)

Thank You, Redeemer, for allowing me to be an instrument of Your peace.

How Elder Mediation Works

There are a small but growing number of mediators who specialize in elder affairs. Their job is to "help resolve disputes, typically outside a courtroom," according to Glenn Ruffenach, an editor with *The Wall Street Journal,* writing in *Smart Money.*

These mediators "help families work through concerns and fights involving caregiving, inheritance, living arrangements, estate planning and related issues."

Elder mediation is hard work, but it can help families learn to work together to solve problems. "Success usually depends on a seemingly simple, yet frequently difficult, task: hearing out and weighing others' viewpoints," notes Barbara Sunderland Manousso, founder of a mediation network in Houston.

Calmly hearing out and weighing other people's viewpoints is good advice for creating peaceful relationships at any age.

One who forgives an affront fosters friendship, but one who dwells on disputes will alienate a friend. (Proverbs 7:19)

Lord, help us to resolve family disputes in a respectful and caring manner.

The Holy Hurricane of Family Life

Lay evangelist Bill Donaghy once wrote a prayer for overwhelmed parents. Here are some excerpts:

"Father, Son, Spirit, Three-fold Family from Whom all families are founded. Help us this day to rejoice in the chaos that is our family. To enter intentionally into the endless mystery of the exhausting energy and tempestuous roller coaster ride of our children's emotions…"

"Bless our family, these tired hearts and tiny hands, and help us all. Give us this day the daily bread of patience and peace, for this time shall pass, and these little ones and we will be weathered by greater storms than these…"

"May we find You in these Gifts, in this Present, in these miracles, all. May we find Your Peace, not apart from this Holy Hurricane of family life, seeking outside a solitary shelter, but may we dance in the very Center of this Holy Communion of Persons, in the Eye of this Sanctifying Storm, this Holy Place, where saints may be formed, and the dross of our sin and weakness burned away, till only gold remains. Amen."

Love the family of believers. (1 Peter 2:17)

Thank You for the gift of my family, Father.

Address Your Feelings, Grow Closer to God

Every one of us, at one time or another, has been overwhelmed by feelings of loneliness, anger or betrayal. Father John Rose, pastoral leader of St. Vincent de Paul Church in Syracuse, New York, insists that it is our acknowledgment of these feelings that brings us closer to the Son of God.

"Jesus has told us to love our enemy," he writes in *The Catholic Sun*. "Sometimes the 'enemy' may be distrust of our feelings. By befriending our feelings we may discover that they are wearing the disguise of Jesus who wishes to speak to us through them."

"By ignoring our feelings, we give them more power," Father John concludes. "It is important for our spiritual journey that we take time to listen to their message…Loneliness or any other of our feelings are invitations to a deeper, more personal relationship with Jesus, with ourselves and with our friends."

May we always embrace our feelings, inasmuch as they bring us closer to God.

Come to Me, all you that are weary…and I will give you rest. (Matthew 11:28)

Jesus, may we use our feelings to grow closer to You.

Prayer for Protection of Religious Liberty

In these ever-changing times, it is important to protect our freedom of religion. Here, in part, is a prayer from the U.S. Conference of Catholic Bishops website invoking God's help:

"O God our Creator, from Your provident hand we have received our right to life, liberty and the pursuit of happiness. You have called us as Your people and given us the right and the duty to worship You, the only true God, and Your Son, Jesus Christ.

"Through the power and working of Your Holy Spirit, You call us to live out our faith in the midst of the world, bringing the light and the saving truth of the Gospel to every corner of society.

"We ask You to bless us in our vigilance for the gift of religious liberty. Give us the strength of mind and heart to readily defend our freedoms when they are threatened; give us courage in making our voices heard on behalf of the rights of Your Church and the freedom of conscience of all people of faith. We ask this through Christ our Lord. Amen."

For freedom Christ has set us free.
(Galatians 5:1)

Abba, help us to be strong warriors for our faith.

The Responsibility of Freedom

In his writings, founding father Benjamin Franklin offered many valuable insights about government and the citizenry. Here are a few:

- "A nation of well-informed men who have been taught to know and prize the rights which God has given them cannot be enslaved. It is in the religion of ignorance that tyranny begins."
- "Only a virtuous people are capable of freedom. As nations become more corrupt...they have more need of masters."
- "The Constitution only gives people the right to pursue happiness. You have to catch it yourself."
- "Freedom is not a gift bestowed upon us by other men, but a right that belongs to us by the laws of God and nature."

A notable thing about Franklin's quotes is that they put a responsibility on the average citizen. Too often, we think that politicians can solve all our problems. And it's true that they can help—or hurt. But our society falls or rises based on the choices each of us makes in our daily lives. Choose wisely.

Do not use your freedom as an opportunity for self-indulgence. (Galatians 5:13)

Lord, help me conform my will to Yours.

Outcasts United

Even though they'd endured war and genocide in countries like Bosnia, Sudan and Iraq, life in the housing projects of Clarkston, Georgia wasn't easy for the children and teens whose refugee families were resettled there.

Enter Jordanian immigrant Luma Mufleh, a woman who saw that these young people needed an alternative to gang life, which was growing in popularity because it made them feel protected and like they were a part of something bigger than themselves.

Under Mufleh's tough-but-caring tutelage, the kids created a soccer team called The Fugees, developed a sense of team spirit and personal responsibility, and overcame the prejudiced attitudes of some locals.

The Christopher Award-winning young adult book *Outcasts United* shares this true story about the power of role models—and one coach's attempt to build community out of diversity.

The alien who resides with you shall be to you as the citizen. (Leviticus 19:34)

Help me be welcoming to strangers, God of all.

Developing Your "Sheep Smarts"

There has always been a competition between the intelligence garnered by "street smarts" versus "book smarts." Father Mark Sietsema adds a third kind of aptitude all Christians should possess: "sheep smarts."

"Typically, we don't think about sheep as intelligent animals," Father Mark writes in *The Orthodox Observer*. "But when it comes to the flock of Christ, sheep smarts are one of the goals of Christian life. When [Orthodox Christians] are baptized, the priest prayed that you would be made a 'provaton loyikon'…Literally, it means a 'logical sheep'…A logical sheep would both save his own skin and warn other sheep of danger."

In other words, a reasonable sheep or member of the Lord's flock would be loving but discerning, generous but wise. This person would utilize their "book" or "street" smarts to more actively develop their "sheep smarts."

"The scholar can be the scribe with a storehouse of intellectual treasures that raises us up from our sheep-like gullibility," Father Mark Sietsema concludes.

See, I am sending you out like sheep…so be wise as serpents and innocent as doves. (Matthew 10:16)

Jesus, help us to both learn and teach Your ways.

The Singing Nurse

Growing up with a talent and passion for singing, Jared Axen performed internationally with various choirs, earned a degree in music, and trained with a vocal coach. Yet when the time came to pursue a career, he chose nursing.

Though Axen didn't intend to integrate music with medicine, he couldn't help but sing to himself while working at Henry Mayo Newhall Memorial Hospital in Santa Clarita Valley, California. Patients who overheard him asked him to sing more. His approach soon became so popular that he received the Southern California Hospital Hero Award in 2012 for his unique way of touching patients' lives.

Why does Axen think his approach is so popular? He told HometownStation.com, "In the medical field, you're working with somebody who is going through a very stressful time in their life...And they're used to...being treated as patients rather than as people. Music and singing is a common language. It lets you be able to bond with somebody on a very different level."

How can you bond with the people in your life?

Awake, awake, utter a song! (Judges 5:12)

Inspire us with the beauty of music, Holy Redeemer.

Faith Through the Storm

Aura Marina Meza looked out the back door of her Howard Beach, New York apartment the night of Hurricane Sandy, and saw that it was windy, but not raining. When she turned around to return to her living room, she was met by a powerful rush of icy water so high that it covered her kitchen stove. Then the lights went out. She found shelter with a neighbor on the second floor, but her apartment and possessions were destroyed.

Thankfully, Meza's family and friends have given her material and emotional support—and her son moved her into his Long Island home until her apartment can be renovated. Though she lost everything and now has a two-hour commute to her cleaning job in Brooklyn, Meza remains positive.

She told the *Daily News,* "Sometimes I get depressed...But God made me strong, and my children are taking care of me. If God takes away all the things I had, it is because He is going to bring better things to me. I don't look back, I have to look to the future. I'm going to fly like the eagle."

In the shadow of Your wings I will take refuge, until the destroying storms pass by. (Psalm 57:1)

Help me weather the storms of life, Jesus.

And They Call it Puppy Love

Mark Gaffey, 52, and Claire Johnson, 50, a blind couple from Stoke-on-Trent, England, recently announced their engagement on a television special called *Me and My Guide Dog*. Interestingly enough, it was Mark and Claire's two guide dogs, Rodd and Venice, who first became a couple. These two amorous golden retrievers met when their owners took a guide dog training course in Shrewsbury.

"[The dogs] were always playing together," Mark told *The Staffordshire Sentinel*. "The trainers said they were the love and romance of the course, and they brought us together."

Even after their training sessions with their dogs had ended, Claire and Mark got together many times, each outing growing progressively longer than the last. It soon became clear that love was in the air—and not just for Rodd and Venice.

"[Mark and I] connected straightaway," Claire adds. "We chatted about everything and anything...And it wouldn't have happened if it wasn't for our dogs."

Let us love one another, for love is from God. (1 John 4:7)

Christ, may we welcome love at every stage of our lives.

The Roots of Courage

In Florence, Italy, July 1944, Tour de France champion Gino Bartali faced torture and death at the hands of Major Mario Carita. Though the military officer's last name meant "charity," his idol was brutal killer Heinrich Himmler, the Nazi leader in charge of Hitler's Gestapo and SS.

Why was Bartali, a major Italian celebrity, being interrogated? As revealed in Aili and Andres McConnon's Christopher Award-winning biography *Road to Valor*, the devout Catholic secretly helped save Jews from the Italian holocaust.

Bullied as a child because he was small for his age, Bartali identified with the underdog. He came to mistrust the Fascist government after a colleague of his father was killed for trying to gain basic rights for workers. Bartali also came to befriend a Jewish immigrant from Russia, Giacomo Goldenberg, who fled to Italy to escape persecution in his homeland.

All these experiences in his youth lay the groundwork for the heroic actions Bartali would take during one of Italy's darkest periods. More of the story tomorrow.

Give me wisdom and knowledge.
(2 Chronicles 1:10)

Jesus, grant me the wisdom to recognize injustice.

Faith versus Oppression

Gino Bartali's success as a cyclist in Italy coincided with the rise in power of Fascist leader Benito Mussolini. Bartali, however, resisted becoming a tool of the regime because the Catholic faith he had practiced since boyhood stood in stark contrast to Fascist principles.

Whereas Mussolini shut down Catholic sports clubs and the Boy Scouts because he feared the religion's influence, Bartali attended Mass regularly, prayed daily, and read about saints like Anthony of Padua. This didn't go over well with the Fascist press who mocked Bartali's piety. They couldn't stop covering him, though, because he won races.

Though Bartali felt devastated when World War II derailed his sports career during his athletic prime, the situation led to a much darker reality for Italy's Jews, especially when Mussolini joined forces with Hitler in 1943. Gino Bartali knew he wanted to help the Jewish people—even if it cost him his life.

The conclusion of the story tomorrow.

**Walk before Me...keeping My statutes.
(2 Chronicles 7:17)**

Give me the strength to hold true to Your laws, Lord.

A Humble Hero

At the request of his friend, Cardinal Elia Dalla Costa, Tour de France champion Gino Bartali joined a secret network of freedom fighters who would deliver forged identity documents to Italian Jews and refugees hoping to escape imprisonment or death. He did this by smuggling the documents inside his bicycle.

Bartali also hid his old friend, Giacomo Goldenberg, and his family in an apartment he bought with his cycling winnings.

With all that clandestine activity, it's no surprise that Fascist Major Mario Carita grew suspicious of Bartali, threatening him with torture and death if he didn't reveal what he knew about Jews in hiding. Despite being inwardly nervous, Bartali played it cool during his interrogation and lived to continue his work.

By the time World War II ended, Bartali's actions had saved hundreds of Jewish lives. But he never publicized this fact because he felt it would be bragging. On May 5, 2000, Gino Bartali died. Aili and Andres McConnon's 2012 biography *Road to Valor* chronicles the extent of his wartime heroism for the first time so his story can inspire future generations.

Hate evil and love good. (Amos 5:15)

Help me be a champion for the persecuted, Savior.

'Please God, Don't Let Me Forget'

How many times have we promised not to take our blessings for granted? But oftentimes, despite our best intentions, it takes a groundbreaking incident or, as in Louanne Payne's case, a life-altering trip to Uganda, to make us appreciate the simpler things in life.

"I was so happy to again be seeing my dear friend, Father Titus Ahabyona, and realizing a dream we had discussed for many years become a reality," Payne told the *Western Kentucky Catholic*. "Everywhere we went...we were met by a hardworking people who were filled with joy, faithfulness, and immense pride...Why wasn't I more joyful, faithful, and proud?"

Indeed, these Ugandans do not possess the amenities we take for granted in America, like working electricity or even the ability to celebrate Mass every week. Yet according to Payne, they still live their lives in undeniable joy.

"I am thankful to God that my 16 days experiencing the beauty of the country, spirit and people of Uganda has changed my life forever," Payne concludes. "I hope the changes last."

Happy are the people who...exult in Your name all day long, and extol Your righteousness. (Psalms 89:15-16)

Messiah, rich or poor, may we appreciate life's benefits.

Pleading Guilty

Many years ago, a conscience-stricken father in Louisville, Kentucky, gave up his driver's license for six months in order to teach his 13-year-old son a lesson. After being arrested for drunken driving, this man overheard his son boasting to a friend, "My dad is going to beat this charge in court."

Shocked by the bad example he had given his own child, the father decided to plead guilty. He was fined, and his driving privileges were suspended for six months. The father said, "I'd rather lose my license and pay a fine than have my boy grow up thinking he can disobey the law."

Parents are the most important teachers that young people have. God meant it that way. Every word and deed of both fathers and mothers has a lasting effect, for better or worse, on impressionable young minds.

Help parents realize the great privilege and responsibility entrusted to them by the Lord, and you will be helping create a more peaceful world.

Show yourself in all respects a model of good works, and in your teaching show integrity. (Titus 2:7)

Holy Spirit, instill parents with integrity and wisdom.

Pillows of Love

For 10-year-old Autumn Blinn of Rome, New York, the tradition began when her grandfather, John Santiago, started kidney dialysis treatment a couple of years ago. She designed and made a pillow for him, one he liked so much that he "showed it around." Soon those people were clamoring for pillows of their own.

"Grandpa," said Autumn, "I'll make you all the pillows you want." That was 300 pillows ago, and she's still at it.

Autumn has formed Pillows of Love, and she gives them all away—to local hospitals, even to the Ronald McDonald House in New York City. Some have floral patterns, some have butterflies. They have a way of making kids feel better, because, as Autumn says, they're "really comforting."

When she was honored by her favorite baseball team, the New York Yankees, the *New York Post* quoted manager, Joe Girardi as saying, "To me this is special because it's kids helping kids. It's amazing what this little girl has done. The maturity of her and how she understands what life is really about."

For we are what He has made us, created in Christ Jesus for good works. (Ephesians 2:10)

Jesus, may our good works touch many lives.

Literature and Medicine

There's reading for pleasure. And there's reading for work. Sometimes they can go together, and that's exactly what people at Mercy Medical Center in Baltimore are finding out. They're the local members of "Literature and Medicine: Humanities at the Heart of Health Care," and they're busy practicing what they preach—or, more accurately, practicing what they read.

All the titles in the series are health care-related, and they have hospital personnel working together as they never have before. Franciscan Sister Carole Rybicki, a Mercy chaplain, says the program has forged stronger relationships between departments. "We get to know each other on a whole different level," she points out. "Ultimately, we're all in this together. We're working for the patients, and we all have different roles."

A story by Maria Wiering in *The Catholic Review*, Baltimore's archdiocesan newspaper, pointed out that some of the book titles are assigned for reading in a given month, while others are there for the taking. As one participant explained: "It makes you stretch!"

Wisdom is as good as an inheritance. (Ecclesiastes 7:11)

God, increase our academic and spiritual learning.

Toward a Peaceful Life

The world around us is often filled with chaos and confusion. How does one find peace in the midst of messaging and movement? One website suggested some ways to stop the stress, and start the serene:

- Commit to change—and take control. Knowing where you are going, and how you'll best get there is a good first step.
- Don't be so hard on yourself—love yourself instead! Nothing stops inner peace more than judging your own mistakes too harshly. Remember, you are not a superhero.
- Cut off negative people. They are not helping you be the best person, living the best life.
- Face your fears. A state of worry hinders a peace-filled life. Be realistic about what might happen, and be logical in planning ways to deal with those difficult times.

And remember, a bit of the Lord's own peace is just a prayer away.

May the Lord give strength to His people! May the Lord bless His people with peace! (Psalm 29:11)

Lord, help me to spread Your peace to all I meet this day.

A Life-Saving Accident

On July 23, 2013, Duane Innes of Kent, Washington, was driving a minivan to a Mariners-Red Sox baseball game with his children. Innes, 48, moved into the carpool lane, when a pickup truck suddenly cut across two lanes of traffic in front of him, just missing the concrete divider. Innes sideswiped the vehicle and noticed as he looked back that the driver was passed out.

"The best-case scenario is I need to match his speed, get in front of him and let him hit me," Innes, a fighter jet manager at Boeing, recalled thinking to the *Seattle Times.*

The driver of the pickup, 80-year-old retired store owner Bill Pace, had suffered a heart attack two days earlier and fainted due to poor circulation, his foot still on the accelerator. Pace and his insurance company, State Farm, which agreed to cover Innes's car damages, are grateful for the latter's intervention.

"We wish to thank you [Innes] for the actions you took to save Bill's life," State Farm's Clayton Ande wrote. "State Farm and the Pace family consider you to be a hero. I wish there were more people like you in the world."

Little children, let us love...in...action.
(1 John 3:18)

God, may we seize every opportunity to help others.

Redeeming a Tragic Day

July 20, 2012, is remembered as a tragic day because of the movie theater shooting which killed 12 people and injured 58 others in Aurora, Colorado. But Eugene Han and Kirstin Davis chose to take back that day for a joyous purpose: specifically, their wedding.

Han was with Davis in the theater that night, and endured gunshot wounds to his knee and hip while protecting her. His recovery lasted several months, during which time the couple, who had dated for three years, grew closer. Han told *ABC News,* "When the theater shooting happened, that's when I was like, 'I really need to do this because you don't know what's going to happen after tomorrow.'"

The wedding took place on July 20, 2013, at Village East Baptist Church in Aurora. The minister called the day "happy and sacred," a perfect description for an event that replaces a memory of death with the reality of redemption and new life.

He is the source of your life in Christ Jesus, who became for us wisdom from God, and righteousness and sanctification and redemption. (1 Corinthians 1:30)

Lord, redeem the tragic elements of our lives.

A Humble Man

When astronaut Neil Armstrong died in 2012, many people remembered his history-making walk on the moon. Yet Armstrong himself was never comfortable with that fame. His wife, Janet, once said, "He feels guilty that he got all the acclaim for an effort of tens of thousands of people."

Following Armstrong's passing, Patheos.com blogger Karen Spears Zacharias wrote about the astronaut's humility: "Armstrong was a product of another culture...a culture in which bragging about one's self, in any form, was considered the height of rudeness...Flaunting wealth or one's success was something only the crass or simply ignorant would do."

Zacharias concluded, "Armstrong said that landing on the moon and looking back at earth did not make him feel like a giant among men. Instead, he said, it made him feel very, very small...Acknowledging how very, very small we are is the first step toward recognizing our position before God and the wide-open universe."

The heavens are telling the glory of God; and the firmament proclaims His handiwork. (Psalm 19:1)

Make me humble, O Lord.

Holy Water Revives Child Actor

Lucy Hussey-Bergonzi, a 13-year-old actress with a small role in *Harry Potter and the Half-Blood Prince,* suffered a brain hemorrhage after shooting the film in England in 2009. The hemorrhage was caused by a rare condition she had since birth.

After five days on life support, doctors told her parents that she would not survive, and it was time to say goodbye to their daughter. Soon after, Lucy's mother Denise told her husband Robert that they needed to have Lucy baptized. "At that point," Denise told the *Daily Mail,* "I thought she was going to die and I wanted to give her the best chance in the next life."

The family gathered to pray for Lucy, and the priest placed holy water on her forehead. Suddenly, Lucy's arm shot up in the air. They thought she was having a fit, but within 24 hours, Lucy was taken off life support and was recovering on her own. She spent several years reclaiming her health, and re-learning how to talk, walk, and eat. Doctors can't explain what happened or why, but the consensus is this: it is a miracle that Lucy is alive.

I have baptized you with water; but He will baptize you with the Holy Spirit. (Mark 1:8)

In impossible times, let us bring ourselves to the Lord.

Generous in Forgiveness

They were just three words, but they spoke volumes. "I forgive you," said the Rev. Varius Valnord, and with that message Andrew Kelly found a measure of relief. But Kelly still faced a life of sad remorse.

Andrew Kelly, who had been a member of the New York Police Department, pleaded guilty to drunkenly mowing down the Rev. Valnord's 32-year-old daughter, Vionique. Facing time in jail and five years of probation, he surprised the minister and extended his hand as he said, "I'm sorry for what happened."

That was when the Rev. Valnord, pastor of the Haitian Church of God in Brooklyn, delivered his brief message. "I forgive you," he said. He added: "I don't want any more pain to be caused to anybody." Said Kelly later to his lawyer: "It was more generous than I could have imagined."

As the Rev. Valnord explained it to the *Daily News,* "I believe in forgiveness, and I believe that after they put him away in jail all the rest is in God's hands."

And be kind to one another, tenderhearted, forgiving one another. (Ephesians 4:32)

Father, release us from the prisons of our grudges.

Finding Faith at the Mall

Clergy members speak often of the gift of presence. Many times, they say, people will thank them for "just being there" at a moment of need. That being the case, a Carmelite priest named Brice Riordan exercised that gift more than most.

For 40 years until his death in 2010, he tended to the needs of shoppers and store workers at one of New Jersey's largest and busiest shopping malls. He enjoyed his ministry, as an obituary by Jay Levin in *The Record* of Hackensack pointed out. And the priest who succeeded him in the mall's chapel explained why:

"He was a compassionate individual who could listen to people at any level they wanted to speak, and always conveyed to them that they were heard."

Father Riordan didn't just stay in the chapel; he went out and met people and listened to their stories. He became familiar to thousands, especially in the bustling holiday season.

As Levin wrote, he was as much a fixture at the mall as sale days at a big department store—and he loved every minute of it.

Do not worry about tomorrow. (Matthew 6:31)

Heavenly Father, may we treasure the present as the true gift it is.

I'll Take the Meteorite Ring

What is today a practical, yet dull metal, iron was to the ancient Egyptians so much more.

"Iron was a rare and beautiful material which, as it fell from the sky, surely had some magical/religious properties," offers researcher Joyce Tyldesley, an Egyptologist at the University of Manchester in England.

The discovery of an ancient Egyptian iron bead inside a 5,000-year-old tomb, crafted from a meteorite, wasn't an isolated cosmic find for scientists. German researchers had already found a heavy Buddha statue dating back to the eighth and 10th centuries that had been carved from a meteorite.

What we value in material things may change. What remains forever priceless—God's love for us and our love for one another.

My children, be true to your training and be at peace; hidden wisdom and unseen treasure—of what value is either? (Sirach 41:14)

You bless us with all good things, Father; to You we give thanks.

Living Frugally

Making ends meet is a struggle for many people, and that's certainly been the case for Julie and Rusty Bulloch, a self-employed couple who've welcomed nearly 30 troubled teens to live on their family ranch over the past 16 years. Yet their commitment to taking on extra mouths to feed hasn't wavered.

During an interview on *Christopher Closeup,* Julie said, "We live off the land, we have a garden...and my whole family hunts. That helps a lot with the food bill...[And] when we were struggling...God always provided that extra job that came in."

Julie believes living frugally has had a positive long-term effect on her family, and that it could do the same for others: "There are parents who are working two jobs to make ends meet, but some are doing it to provide things like a pool, someone to take care of the lawn, a maid. Not all, but there are a few. It would be better to cut back on overtime and say, 'We're having peanut butter and jelly for supper. We're going to do family time.' That's one thing you can't buy and never get enough of."

Do not become a beggar by feasting with borrowed money. (Sirach 18:33)

Lord, guide me in using money and resources wisely.

A Surfer's Best Days

Professional surfer Israel "Izzy" Paskowitz has loved the sport since age six when his father first took him out on a board. Izzy hoped to do the same with his son, Isaiah, until the boy was diagnosed with autism at age three. Unable to deal with the news, Izzy traveled constantly and drank heavily until his wife, Danielle, told him to either come home or stay away for good. He chose to be with his family.

In 1996, they were together in Hawaii for a surfing contest when Isaiah began having a tantrum due to sensory overload. Izzy put his son on his surfboard and paddled into the water. He told *Yahoo News*, "A calm came over him. He was...genuinely happy. He was a regular boy out there doing what I always dreamed of doing with him."

That incident led Izzy and Danielle to found Surfers Healing, a free program in which pro surfers ride the waves with autistic children. The program serves 3,000 kids a year around the country—and Izzy's joy remains now that he is spreading it far and wide. He says, "These are the best days of my life."

**He turns a desert into pools of water.
(Psalm 107:35)**

Father, help all parents and children find ways to connect.

A Daughter's Dying Gift

For once, Illinois native Ricardo Cerezo was glad to have his hand caught in the cookie jar—he unearthed a lottery ticket in there worth $4.85 million.

The Cerezos' cookie jar was a gift from their late 14-year-old daughter Savannah, who suffered throughout her short life from frequent seizures. They used the jar for storing family keepsakes and lottery tickets. Ricardo's wife told him to check all their tickets, ensuring that none of them had any value.

"The last ticket said 'file a claim,'" Cerezo told *NBC Chicago* reporter Laura Jiggetts. "Not a congratulations, not an amount, just said 'file a claim.'" Further investigation by Cerezo proved his ticket to be worth a significant amount of money. "The winning ticket couldn't have come at a better time for the family," Jiggetts added. "Cerezo's home in Geneva was facing pending foreclosure."

The family's only regret about their windfall was that their daughter wasn't alive to share it. Still, the Cerezos are grateful for Savannah's last, most precious gift.

For You bless the righteous...with favor. (Psalm 5:12)

Jesus, may we give thinks for life's unexpected miracles.

Find Time For Relationships

"Life is a sacred adventure" write Frederic and Mary Ann Brussat in their comprehensive work, *Spiritual Literacy: Reading the Sacred in Everyday Life*. Relationships are crucial to that adventure since they "form the spiritual web of our lives...Our deepest values are expressed through these essential bonds."

The authors offer an illustrative story from Rabbi Harold Kushner's book *When All You've Ever Wanted Isn't Enough*.

Kushner watched a boy and girl working hard building an elaborate sand castle on the beach, complete with towers, moats and gates. Just before they finished it a huge wave swept it away. He expected the children would be devastated and in tears. "Instead, they ran up...away from the water, laughing and holding hands" and started building anew.

Kushner took away the lesson that when life's waves inevitably knock down our projects, "only the person who has somebody's hand to hold will be able to laugh."

If you have come to me in friendship, to help me, then my heart will be knit to you. (1 Chronicles 12:17)

Show us how to deepen our relationships, Lord.

An Instrument to Bless the World With

One day many years ago, Fritz Kreisler, a famous violinist, walked into an old antique shop. From a room in the rear of the store, he heard someone playing a violin. He asked to see the instrument so he could examine it. Then he offered to buy it.

The shopkeeper told him that it had been sold to a collector who planned to place it in his small museum. Determined to secure the violin, Kreisler sought out the collector and unsuccessfully tried to persuade him to sell his latest acquisition.

Finally, the collector allowed Kreisler to play the violin. Kreisler admitted to playing "as one condemned to death would have played to obtain ransom" because he felt "that it was not an antique to look at, but an instrument to bless the world with."

When Kreisler finished playing, the collector told him, "I have no right to keep it. It belongs to you. Go out into the world and let it be heard."

God has given each of us at least one talent. Make sure you use it to bless the world.

Go into all the world and proclaim the good news. (Mark 16:15)

Inspire me to share the talents You gave me, Father.

From the Orphanage to the Stage

Michaela DePrince's childhood in Sierra Leone, Africa, didn't suggest a promising future: her father was murdered, her mother starved to death, and the girl was abused by workers in the orphanage where she went to live.

Michaela found one small comfort when the wind blew a magazine through the orphanage gate one day. On the cover was a ballerina. Captivated by the beauty of the dance and the dancer, Michaela held onto that cover as a source of inspiration.

When she was eventually adopted by a New Jersey couple, Elaine and Charles DePrince, she brought that magazine cover with her. Her new parents discovered her passion and enrolled her in ballet class. With focused determination, Michaela applied herself to dancing. Now 18 years old, she belongs to the Dance Theatre of Harlem and has performed at Lincoln Center.

Regarding the people who hurt her, Michaela told the *Daily News,* "I realize every single day how lucky I am to be here...Forgiving those people gives me the chance to move on."

Do justice for the orphan and the oppressed. (Psalm 10:18)

Thank You for bringing light out of the darkness, Lord.

'We Had No Idea What We Were Taking'

On the night of July 31, 2013, a group of robbers broke into California's San Bernardino County Sexual Assault Services, which helps victims of sexual abuse. In addition to cutting wires to disable the building's complex alarm system, the thieves stole six computers, a laptop and a bag of valuables.

Executive director Candy Stallings was surprised when she arrived at the office the next day—but not because of the robbery. "All my stuff was in the front door," Candy told *NBC Los Angeles*. "There was a shopping cart, and there were the PCs that were taken. There was the laptop. Everything was there."

An investigator found a note from the robbers on the keyboard of the laptop that read: "We had no idea what we were taking. Here is your stuff back. We hope you guys can continue to make a difference in people's lives. God bless."

Apparently, the burglars regretted their crime when they realized what they had stolen, showing that a person's conscience is a powerful thing.

Repent therefore, and turn to God. (Acts 3:19)

Father, may we strive to cleanse ourselves of all iniquities.

The King of Queens on the King of Kings

Best known for his popular sitcom *The King of Queens,* actor Kevin James has been making people laugh for years as a stand-up comic and actor. As he's gotten older and become a husband and father himself, the 47-year-old has more deeply embraced the Catholic faith with which he was raised.

James told *Catholic News Service,* "I've been very guilty, a lot, of not knowing my faith too much and just praying when I needed it—when something bad happened in my life, and not being thankful when things turned good. The more I realize how important it is, the more I want to learn about it and do the right thing. All good is from [God], and so I want to honor Him. It's honestly about learning more and instilling that in my kids and my friends, and those around me."

We often treat our religion as if it was a shallow pond instead of a deep well. But its life-sustaining wisdom and graces are there for everyone with an open mind, heart, and soul. Dive deeply into the riches of your faith.

Give me understanding that I may keep Your law and observe it with my whole heart. (Psalm 119:34)

May I always pursue my journey toward You, Lord.

Mightier Than the Sword

The cruelest, most violent Samurai in Japan decides he wants to become enlightened. He bursts into the home of an esteemed Zen Master and demands that the Master teach him how to become enlightened.

The Zen Master looks deeply into his eyes and says, "No. You are a dirty, vicious Samurai. I will not teach you."

Enraged, the Samurai yanks out his sword and places it right at the Zen Master's neck. He hollers, "Do you have any idea who I am? I am the cruelest Samurai in the world! I can cut your throat and not blink an eye."

Without skipping a beat, the Master calmly responds, "Do you have any idea who I am? I can let you slit my throat and not blink an eye."

The Samurai falls to his knees, sobbing, overcome by the presence of a man mightier than his sword.

He was oppressed, and he was afflicted, yet he did not open his mouth; like a lamb that is led to the slaughter, and like a sheep that before its shearers is silent, so he did not open his mouth. (Isaiah 53:7)

Help me to be a force for peace amidst violence, Jesus.

Before Each Meal

Whether at a hurried breakfast at home, sitting at a lunch counter, or before a banquet at the Waldorf, many make it a practice to pause a moment and ask God's blessing.

Countless millions over the earth say this age-old prayer: "Bless us, O Lord, and these Thy gifts which we are about to receive from Thy bounty, through Christ our Lord, Amen."

A prayer such as this is a simple, forceful reminder that the all-powerful Creator is the Author of all that we are, and the loving Provider of every mouthful of food we eat.

This brief prayer, said three times a day, will not only keep us aware of the Divine Presence, but will prompt us to share the peace and joy of Christ with the world as far as we can reach.

It will help us to lift our minds and hearts above the distractions and temptations of daily life and keep them focused on the reason for our existence.

My mouth will speak the praise of the LORD, and all flesh will bless His holy name forever and ever. (Psalm 145:21)

Keep us ever conscious of Your abiding presence, O Lord.

Consoler of Struggling Souls

It started simply enough: Father Jean-Baptiste Marie Vianney had been ordained a Catholic priest, and in addition to his other duties he heard confessions. This was in the little French town of Ars, not all that far from where he had been born in 1786. "Have you heard about Father Jean?" his parishioners soon exclaimed. "He gives wonderful advice to his penitents!"

Indeed he did. Soon the word was spreading—beyond Ars, beyond his diocese, eventually to all of France itself. Father Jean was wonderful in the confessional, giving advice, preaching the word of God. Before long he was spending hour after hour hearing confessions, ultimately devoting up to 18 hours a day in the confessional, just to console struggling souls.

We know him today as St. John Vianney, the Curé of Ars—canonized a saint in 1925, the patron of all parish priests, whose memorial is observed on August 4. His life made a remarkable difference, and he stands as a model for all priests to this day.

If another disciple sins, you must rebuke the offender, and if there is repentance, you must forgive. (Luke 17:3)

Lord, may we always make room in our lives for forgiveness, towards others and ourselves.

Surviving the Widow Maker

It was just an ordinary day saving lives for Detroit paramedic Joseph Hardman until his was the life that needed saving.

While performing CPR on a heart attack patient during the ambulance ride to the hospital, Hardman experienced what he described as "a sudden explosion-like feeling in my chest." Regardless, he continued working on his patient until they arrived at the ER, where both of them received immediate, life-saving treatment.

Hardman's type of heart blockage is known as a "widow maker" because it is located in a key artery. If he hadn't already been en route to the hospital, he likely would have died. One of his doctors told reporters that the odds of such a thing happening are "one in a million."

Thankfully, both patients' lives were saved that day due to Hardman's unwavering dedication to his job—and a few special blessings from above.

Let us run with perseverance the race that is set before us. (Hebrews 12:1)

Strengthen our hearts physically and spiritually, Lord.

Secret Prayers

"They said God didn't exist. I couldn't come to church or pray or speak of God at all," recalled 76-year-old Maria Dhimitri to *Catholic News Service* about her years growing up under communism.

Dhimitri was raised in a Catholic family in Shkoder, Albania, which was ruled by a communist regime after World War II. At first, they just made going to church difficult, but in 1967, they banned religion altogether, making Albania the world's first "constitutionally atheist state."

"All the priests were arrested and killed, or put in jail," said Dhimitri, who never stopped praying in the privacy of her own home—though even there she had to be careful because, under the communists, the "walls have ears."

When communism fell in Albania during the early 1990s, the few churches that remained were repaired over time and reopened. Today, Dhimitri is the regular organist at Sacred Heart Catholic Church, providing her fellow believers with the beauty of faith and music they missed for so many years.

In the world you face persecution. But take courage; I have conquered the world! (John 16:33)

Help us stay faithful to You always, Jesus.

In Memory of Adam

After attending Saturday evening Mass, Steve and Lisa Gott were at their home in suburban Minneapolis when they got the call that every parent fears the most: one of their son's friends said simply, "Adam had an accident." By the time they got to the hospital, two hours away, Adam had died.

Their son, who had just finished his freshman year in college, was riding a motorbike when he hit a tree. Despite wearing a helmet, the impact of the blow to the head proved fatal. That was in 2012, and naturally Steve and Lisa Gott still mourn their loss. But something happened last year that helped to raise their spirits—a lacrosse tournament in Adam's memory.

Adam had been a lacrosse standout in high school, and his old coaches organized the tourney. Nine high school teams took part, and more than $20,000 was raised for scholarships. The Gotts were jubilant. "Adam would be thrilled to know that there's funding now available to help college students," said Steve. And Lisa added, "He'd have been thrilled to see everyone having so much fun."

Righteousness delivers from death.
(Proverbs 11:4)

Divine Savior, may my actions bring comfort to the grieving.

The Best and Worst of Times

Marriage is a happy institution and an eternal bond. When one takes the vows, it's a joyous occasion. That joy continues, but pain often arises when two broken people stumble toward Heaven together. It's the tough times that make marriage vows important: the sick times, the sad times, the weak times.

That's why marriage is a sacrament that encompasses both life and death. Sacraments are sacrifices; something good exchanged for something more wonderful. In marriage, two people do more than love: they serve each other. And moreover, by serving each other, married couples serve their children, their family, and their community.

Through service, marriage gives testimony to the love of Christ, who served us on Earth through His ministry and by suffering death. Unless couples die to self in marriage, no fruit can be borne from their love. It is in the light of love that shadows are seen and Christ is fully realized: it is in being prepared to die for one's spouse that one can truly live and love.

Live in love, as Christ loved us and gave Himself up for us. (Ephesians 5:2)

Lord, give me the strength to love and serve my spouse.

Terror Doesn't Have to Win

Following the 2013 terrorist attack on the Boston Marathon, a co-worker of *Verily* magazine contributor Amanda Fazzio said, "There's going to come a time when people just stay inside."

That got Fazzio thinking about ways to regain peace after times of trauma. Her suggestions include:

- "Don't focus on the horror. Instead of dwelling on the pain and suffering of others, focus your mental energies on reaching out to those who are suffering. Nothing cures mental agony like action."

- "When terrorist events occur, the media inundate us with all of the horrible details. Try to redirect your focus on the beautiful displays of human compassion and goodness that always surface after tragedy."

- "Physical action helps release the tension and ease some of the sense of helplessness. Volunteer somewhere in your community and allow yourself to be moved by the fact that, in serving, you are part of a larger movement of people striving for good."

Put away violence and oppression. (Ezekiel 45:9)

Bring us comfort and healing, Spirit of Peace.

A Mother's Quick Thinking

Eight-year-old Ian McGreevy was enjoying a Saturday afternoon playing baseball in Harrington Park, New Jersey, when his life almost came to an end. A thrown ball accidentally hit him in the chest, causing him to collapse.

Maureen Reneghan, the mother of a player on the opposing team, rushed to Ian and discovered that he wasn't breathing and his heart had stopped beating. At first she performed chest compressions, but they weren't helping so she tried mouth-to-mouth resuscitation. The boy's heart finally started beating again.

As a mother herself, Reneghan feels especially grateful that she was able to save another mom from going through the greatest grief possible: the death of a child. She told *Eyewitness News*, "I want to see [Ian] playing and running and being happy because I'll never forget his face and I'll love him forever."

Strength and dignity are her clothing, and she laughs at the time to come. She opens her mouth with wisdom, and the teaching of kindness is on her tongue. (Proverbs 31:25-26)

Holy Spirit, guide us during times of trouble.

Nurturing Untapped Potential

Yusuf Randera-Rees seemed to be living the American dream. The South African native, who had attended Harvard and Oxford Universities, was earning a six-figure salary on Wall Street. Yet his own success wasn't fulfilling enough so he returned to his home country to help its citizens meet their untapped potential as entrepreneurs.

As reported by *NBC News*, Randera-Rees established a nonprofit program called The Awethu Project. He interviews and tests applicants to see if they've got the ideas, initiative and determination to create a business; then they receive an initial investment of $1,500. All the businesses he's invested in—like Chris Pienaar's bread delivery service or Lesika Matlou's tour agency—now earn that amount every month.

Randera-Rees is thrilled with the progress of his entrepreneurs. He says, "They're innovative. They want to inspire people in communities like this and that's crucial."

Do what you can to help others reach their potential.

Every generous act of giving, with every perfect gift, is from...the Father of light. (James 1:17)

Teach us to support ourselves while serving others, Lord.

Two Sets of Lungs

As an opera singer, 29-year-old Charity Tillemann-Dick had to train her lungs for years to perform at the height of her abilities. Severe pulmonary hypertension, however, led to those lungs being replaced not once, but twice.

The Washington, D.C. resident traveled to the Cleveland clinic for her first lung transplant. The disease had already taken a toll on her kidneys and liver, which made the already difficult operation that much harder.

As reported by the *Washington Post,* Tillemann-Dick "remained in a medically-induced coma for 34 days," and stayed in the hospital for another two months beyond that. She was able to make her acclaimed Lincoln Center opera debut shortly thereafter, but her new set of lungs soon failed her.

In January 2012, another donor was found. The transplant went smoothly, and Tillemann-Dick was released from the hospital after three weeks. She takes many medications, but remains committed to pursuing her career and loving her family because she knows that no one is guaranteed tomorrow.

The human spirit will endure sickness. (Proverbs 18:14)

Guide us through illnesses, Divine Healer.

I Give It All to God

When suicidal gunman Michael Jordan Hill entered a Decatur, Georgia grammar school, everyone feared it would be another Sandy Hook. The gunman never made it past the front office, though, where he held school bookkeeper Antoinette Tuff (whose last name seems especially appropriate) hostage.

While 800 pre-kindergarten through fifth-grade students from the Ronald E. McNair Discovery Learning Academy managed to be evacuated, Tuff kept the mentally unstable Hill talking. She told him that she loved him, and that killing himself and others was no answer to life's troubles. And though it put her own life more at risk, she also encouraged him to stay with her rather than go outside where she knew he would start shooting kids. In the end, Tuff talked Hill into surrendering. No one was killed.

After an *ABC News* interviewer called her a hero, Tuff responded, "I give it all to God. I'm not a hero. I was terrified. Through His grace and mercy, I kept it together."

**Calmness will undo great offenses.
(Ecclesiastes 10:4)**

In fearful times, O Lord, give us the grace and strength to accomplish Your will.

The Miracle of St. Brigid's

They say that miracles don't happen anymore, but you'll never convince the parishioners of Manhattan's St. Brigid Church. They've seen one happen, and they're sure that all of the Lower East Side is better because it did.

Some years ago their old church had seen better days and was headed for demolition. Fundraising efforts to restore the property fell woefully short, and when determined parishioners turned to legal maneuvers to keep it open they were rejected by the courts. Destruction seemed to be assured.

Then the miracle they'd been praying for actually happened. An anonymous donor stepped forth to make a pledge—a whopping $20 million for the restoration of St. Brigid's; anything left over would go to the parish school. As far as the parishioners were concerned, that qualified as a major-league miracle, and who's to argue?

The rededication of the church has been held, and members of the parish couldn't be happier. They and their neighbors have a miracle to celebrate, one they're reminded of every day.

I know that You can do all things. (Job 42:2)

Paraclete, may we never lose faith in Your divine existence.

The Birth Bus

An old bloodmobile that the owner wanted to turn into a party bus was instead sold to Charlie Rae Young of Tampa Bay, Florida, as a means of offering prenatal care to pregnant women in low-income neighborhoods.

Young, who will soon become a certified midwife, has helped deliver 225 babies since 2010, as a midwife's assistant. Currently the owner of Barefoot Birth pregnancy support services, she realized that women in at-risk communities couldn't always afford vital prenatal care to ensure they have healthy babies. After seeing a mobile clinic that provided immunizations, she thought she could apply the same principle to prenatal care so she bought and renovated the old bus.

As reported by the *Tampa Bay Times,* "Licensed midwives will provide general prenatal checkups, including bimonthly examinations and lab work."

Angela Dunkley, who is supporting the project, said, "With so many people barely making ends meet, this is one steppingstone to a better future for families in need."

Be rich in good works. (1 Timothy 6:18)

Help me find innovative ways to help others, Lord.

Friendships With Substance

When Lisa Schmidt of The Practicing Catholic blog became a stay-at-home mom several years ago, she got involved in various community activities in order to make new friends. Yet these relationships remained superficial, which led Schmidt to a greater yearning for deep, meaningful, spiritual friendships.

She wrote, "Life in our domestic monasteries is often rugged and slippery, and we need sacred friendships to steady our way, to fill our tanks, to encourage, help and lead each other to do good deeds." So how does Schmidt recommend finding these types of friends?

- "Be a good friend with Jesus first. How much time have you wasted with Him lately?"

- "Ask the Lord...to bring us good, holy friends. Make it a daily prayer. And for the friends already in your life, make sure they are a fundamental part of your prayer life."

- "Ask for the intercession of a few saints. I developed a 'board of directors' and asked them to guide my way, to befriend me and coach me how to live."

Faithful friends are life-saving medicine. (Sirach 6:16)

Lead me to those who will lead me to You, Lord.

Saved by Two Jesses

When Hurricane Isaac crashed into Louisiana in August 2012 with winds of up to 80 miles per hour, more than 730,000 residents along the Gulf Coast were left without power.

According to the *Associated Press,* two of the storm's bravest heroes were also two of its worst victims—Jesse Shaffer Sr., age 53, and his son Jesse Jr., 25, of Braithwaite. Despite their home being flooded by 12 feet of water, they both climbed into a free fishing boat and rescued up to 120 people, including babies and several pets.

One of this duo's more amazing rescues involved pulling a family of five off their mobile home roof before it collapsed under water. "They were all on there, screaming their lungs out," Jesse Sr. recounted. "We rescued a lot of people, saw a lot of things you never thought you'd see."

Even in the midst of a tragedy, the goodness of humanity can shine through. May we always be moved to reach out to one another in kindness— no matter what the circumstances.

For You have been a refuge to the poor...a shelter from the rainstorm. (Isaiah 25:4)

Lord, protect us from life's many unpredictable storms.

The Truth Comes Out

Diana Holt can be as persistent as they come, and she proved it when she looked into the case of Edward Lee Elmore. A law student when she started her investigation in 1993, and a full-fledged lawyer when she finished, Holt found that Elmore's was a too-typical case of justice denied to a poor black man.

Elmore, whose court-appointed defense was no match for a hard-charging prosecution, had been found guilty of the 1982 murder of Dorothy Edwards, 76, in Greenwood, South Carolina. Appeals were unsuccessful; Elmore was retried, reconvicted, and once more sentenced to death. Then Holt entered the scene. Her legal work is detailed in *Anatomy of Injustice,* by the Pulitzer Prize-winning writer, Raymond Bonner.

Convinced of his innocence, Holt filed one appeal after another. Finally in 2009, Elmore's sentence was commuted to life. Then, in 2012, after yet another appeal, he walked out of court after 30 years in prison, a free man.

Persistence and truth once again carried the day.

You shall not render an unjust judgment. (Leviticus 19:15)

Holy Judge, may we commit ourselves to justice for all.

Knocking on Heaven's Door

When Scott Simon, the host of NPR's *Weekend Edition Saturday,* sat at his dying mother Patricia's bedside, he shared what was happening on the social media site Twitter. Here are some of his thoughts, filled with grief, grace and humor:

- "I love holding my mother's hand. Haven't held it like this since I was 9. Why did I stop? I thought it unmanly?"

- "Mother cries 'Help Me' at 2:30. Been holding her like a baby since. She's asleep now. All I can do is hold on to her."

- "When she asked for my help last night, we locked eyes. She calmed down. A look of love that surpasses understanding."

- "I know end might be near as this is only day of my adulthood I've seen my mother and she hasn't asked, 'Why that shirt?'"

- "The heavens over Chicago have opened and Patricia Lyons Simon Newman has stepped onstage. She will make the face of heaven shine…As my mother said, the nice thing about being a Chicagoan is she'll continue to be able to vote on Election Day."

Isaac was comforted after his mother's death. (Genesis 24:67)

Comfort the grieving, Destroyer of Death.

A Prayer for Christian Living

Best-selling author Father Jonathan Morris shared a Prayer for Christian Living on his Facebook page. Here is an excerpt:

"Gracious God, we thank You that You reveal Yourself to us in many ways—through Your Word, through the Church, through nature, and through others...Yet, we know that many people, being witnesses to Your goodness and greatness, do not believe. Lord God, we ask You to open our eyes of faith. Enable us to see miracles at work. When times are difficult, help us to see and know that You are there.

"We also know, that in this age of the Church, that You most often work miracles through the hands and feet of those who love You and love others.

"Lord God, I humbly ask You to use me to bring about a miracle—a touch from You—in someone's life. As the apostle Philip listened and obeyed by reaching out to a man in search of grace, (Acts 8:26-39), enable me to hear Your call and to proceed on Your direction. Thank You for what You will do! I am willing. Help Your servant hear Your voice. Amen."

The glory of the Lord shall be revealed. (Isaiah 40:5)

May I walk humbly in Your ways, O Lord.

The Birth of Strength and Courage

In October 2012, the Taliban shot 15-year-old Pakistani schoolgirl Malala Yousafzai for speaking out on behalf of education rights for children, especially girls. Though they meant to assassinate her, Malala survived and became an international symbol for freedom. She addressed the United Nations in July 2013 with the message she wants to spread:

"The terrorists thought that they would change our aims and stop our ambitions but nothing changed in my life except this: Weakness, fear and hopelessness died. Strength, power and courage was born. Dear sisters and brothers, I am not against anyone. Neither am I here to speak in terms of personal revenge. I am here to speak up for the right of education of every child."

"I do not even hate the Talib who shot me. Even if there is a gun in my hand and he stands in front of me, I would not shoot him...This is the philosophy of non-violence that I have learnt from Gandhi Jee, Bacha Khan and Mother Teresa. And this is the forgiveness that I have learnt from my mother and father. This is what my soul is telling me: be peaceful and love everyone."

You save me from violence. (2 Samuel 22:3)

Holy Spirit, instill peace and love in our hearts.

Spiritual Exercises

Sports journalist and runner B.G. Kelley of *St. Anthony Messenger* magazine finds a kind of spirituality in physical activity. He realizes that some people might think of exercise strictly in physical terms, as a way of strengthening muscles and increasing endurance. But it can also keep us connected to God.

Once while running with his wife, Kelley wondered why she slowed up near the end of the race to let her friend beat her. She answered, "It meant more to her to get there first."

Play nurtures the soul, Kelley believes. If we put it into a spiritual context, "it will help us to understand life better, to accept absolute concepts—winning and losing, discipline, hard work. It will reveal character and grace. It will teach respect for limits and laws."

While physical training is of some value, godliness is valuable in every way, holding promise for both the present life and the life to come. (1 Timothy 4:8)

May we not take our physical strength for granted, Jesus.

Grow in Knowledge and Faith at College

For many young people, college is a chance not only to further education, but to assert independence — from both their parents and their childhood religion. According to Sister Margie Lavonis, rather than neglect their faith altogether, Catholic students in particular should utilize the instructive atmospheres of their universities to broaden their knowledge of Catholicism.

"Some students have a great need to explore different faith traditions and I think that is good," Sister Margie acknowledges in *The Catholic Herald*. "However, it is important to include the Catholic Church in that exploration."

Sister Margie offers advice to pupils who are serious about deepening their relationship with God: establish a strong network of "church friends," and find a priest or spiritual mentor to guide them along the difficult but worthwhile road ahead. Above all, she counsels, stay connected to Jesus, for "it is your friendship and faithfulness to Him that will sustain you throughout college and your entire life."

When I was a child, I spoke like a child...when I became an adult, I put an end to childish ways. (1 Corinthians 13:11)

Lord, may we grow in faith throughout our lives.

Holding Out Hope

As head of the Christian Foundation for Children and Aging (CFCA), a Kansas City-based nonprofit, Bob Hentzen walks a lot. In 1996, he walked from Kansas City to Guatemala. More recently, he and his wife Cristina crossed Central and South America raising awareness of poverty, recruiting sponsors and meeting aid recipients.

CFCA provides material assistance to 300,000 people in 22 countries. One former sponsored child, who is now age 25 and completing a social work degree, recalls how the monthly money helped her large family. "There were so many of us, and we had nothing. We didn't know the taste of meat; we ate yellow flour with grease and water."

Hentzen believes his mission goes beyond providing material comfort. He says, "One of the things we can give to these families is this idea: This is a hopeful situation, a powerful worldwide movement, and I belong to it. I can make changes."

Give some of your food to the hungry, and some of your clothing to the naked. (Tobit 4:16)

Inspire us, Holy Spirit, to offer help and hope to those we meet as we travel through life.

Negotiating the Coffee Table

Parents want to protect their children from harm, but small bumps and bruises can provide important lessons. Jennifer Aist suggests the following in her book *Babes in the Woods: Hiking, Camping & Boating with Babies and Young Children:*

"Watch an eight-month-old baby crawl around a coffee table. If left to explore it on his own, he'll run into it a few times...and maybe even get a bit frustrated by it. Very quickly, this same baby will learn to duck going around that coffee table, slow down to avoid crashing into it, and generally learn how to be safe around it."

"The baby with 'hover parents' never has an opportunity to learn by trial and error. So though this baby may never bonk his head on the coffee table at home, he also never develops the skills to avoid bonking his head on any other coffee table. Teach children the skills they need to safely negotiate any coffee table and...you will have taught your child to be capable. Remember, frustration teaches children problem-solving."

It is good for me that I was humbled. (Psalm 119:71)

Protect me from harm as I learn from my mistakes, Lord.

More Than Words

"For every five minutes spent discussing a problem, put in at least 55 minutes of hard work trying to solve it."

That's the advice that Maryknoll Father James Keller, the founder of The Christophers, once sent to an organization that had asked him for suggestions on how to get more effective results out of their meetings.

Both leaders and members felt that they were "too long" on talk, and "too short" on performance.

"From saying to doing is a long step," is the way an old Italian proverb describes the all-too-human tendency to "talk much" and "do little."

It's easy to delude ourselves into thinking that by merely voicing noble principles, passing resolutions and repeating good intentions, we are actually making big headway in changing the world for the better. But wishful thinking counts for little either with God or man. As the Scriptures remind us, we have to back up our words with practical application.

The doers of the law...will be justified. (Romans 2:13)

Inspire me, Holy Spirit, to talk little and do much.

Noah's Endeavor

Though born with cerebral palsy along with minimal hearing and vision, Noah Voelker of Gainesville, Florida, always enjoyed being outdoors and in the company of other people. Since there weren't many opportunities for recreation for the disabled in his area, his parents created Endeavor Recreation.

This charity, now called Noah's Endeavor, allowed Noah and other young people like him to enjoy playing, painting and friendship. His mother Shelly explained the impact the group had on him: "If there's anybody who had a right not to be happy, it was Noah. But he was perfectly happy all the time."

Though he passed away in 2009 at age 19, Noah's legacy lives on through the organization named after him. His life also expanded the already-loving hearts of his parents, who have adopted three special needs children since his death.

The Christophers honored a video about Noah's Endeavor, produced by Shauna Mackey, with first prize in our 2013 Video Contest for College Students.

**The Lord lifts up the downtrodden.
(Psalm 147:6)**

Help us welcome those with special needs, Lord.

Inspiration for the Incarcerated

Deacon Peter Andre, the Director of Prison Ministry for the Diocese of Saint Petersburg, Florida, distributes Christopher materials—such as *Three Minutes a Day* books, Christopher News Notes and prayer cards—to prisoners. He often writes to The Christophers to express his gratitude for the donations, as well as share how they are being used.

Recently, Deacon Peter let us know how important our donations are in their ministry to juvenile offenders. He explained how difficult it is to find religious materials that young people can understand and that will be allowed inside the facilities by Department of Juvenile Justice staff. But he stresses that the Christopher materials are never denied admittance and are very effective at communicating an inspirational message

In his last letter, Deacon Peter wrote: "If we are Christbearers, we can help change the world. This generosity extended to us—to our ministry—has changed the way we reach out to serve the incarcerated! We are truly partners in evangelization and we thank God for your help."

The Lord sets the prisoners free. (Psalm 146:7)

Change the hearts of the incarcerated, Divine Justice.

When Do You Need Courage?

The following entry from the Daily Word website offers some thoughts about the importance of courage:

"I may think of courage as something to summon when danger lurks. Yet at times, I need courage even when no danger or difficulty is apparent. I need courage when unfounded fears cloud my mind and heart. I need courage when I have allowed circumstances to distract me from God's good and ever-present power.

"No matter what has caused my fear, I can look beyond appearances to the reality—to God—and take courage.

"Knowing there is One Presence and One Power gives me the courage to stand strong and release any fears. I know God is present for myself, for my family and friends, and for people all over the world who are facing challenges of any kind."

Be strong and let your heart take courage, all you who wait for the Lord. (Psalm 31:24)

Jesus, may I trust that You are with me through all dangers and troubles. Help me believe Your command, "Do not be afraid."

A Politician's Rehabilitation

It was the summer of 1963 when England's Secretary of State for War, John Profumo, was forced to resign in disgrace after details emerged that he'd had an affair with a Soviet spy.

But as Peggy Noonan recalled in the *Wall Street Journal*, Profumo was genuinely grieved by his own moral lapse and poor judgment. She wrote, "He did the hardest thing for a political figure. He really went away. He went to a place that helped the poor, a rundown settlement house called Toynbee Hall in the East End of London. There he did social work...washing dishes and cleaning toilets. He visited prisons for the criminally insane, helped with housing for the poor and worker education. He worked at Toynbee for 40 years."

Profumo became so admired by the British that upon his death in 2006, the *Daily Telegraph* newspaper wrote, "No one in public life ever did more to atone for his sins; no one behaved with more silent dignity as his name was repeatedly dragged through the mud; and few ended their lives as loved and revered by those who knew him."

Bear fruit worthy of repentance. (Matthew 3:8)

Holy Spirit, help us seek true repentance and contrition.

The Layman's Commandments

An anonymous author composed a list called "The Layman's 10 Commandments." Here are just a few:

- "Prayer is not a 'spare wheel' that you pull out when in trouble, but it is a 'steering wheel' that directs the right path throughout the journey."

- "So why is a car's windshield so large, and the rear view mirror so small? Because our PAST is not as important as our FUTURE. So, look ahead and move on."

- "All things in life are temporary. If going well, enjoy it, they will not last forever. If going wrong, don't worry, they can't last long either."

- "When GOD solves your problems, you have faith in HIS abilities; when GOD doesn't solve your problems, HE has faith in your abilities."

- "A blind person asked St. Anthony: 'Can there be anything worse than losing eyesight?' He replied: 'Yes, losing your vision!'"

**Give heed to His commandments.
(Exodus 15:26)**

You always have my greatest good in mind, Father. Help me trust in and follow Your wisdom.

Use Your Skill to Do His Holy Will

Many years ago, a nurse from Bronxville, New York, sent a brief prayer to Father James Keller, the founder of The Christophers. She hoped he would share it with others so it could help them sanctify their daily tasks as she tries to do.

This is the prayer she wrote:

"Help me, Lord, to use my little skill
As best I can, to do Your holy will.
Give me patience, charity
And, most of all, humility.
Let me find the peace of mind
That comes to those who serve mankind.
And by so doing, serve You too
For this is all I want to do.
Don't let me tire, don't let me shirk,
Give me strength to do my work.
Forgive me if throughout the day,
I don't always take the time to say
The customary prayers to You—
Let my prayer be the work I do."

Pray to the Lord! (Exodus 9:28)

Sustain me in my daily work, Father.

Is Dating OK For My Teen?

If you're the parent of a teen, do you feel you have control over when or whether your youngster starts to date? Rosalind Wiseman, a columnist for *Family Circle* magazine, notes that a too-strict rule against dating might backfire if it results in sneaky behavior. So what is a parent to do?

While you might not be able to manage everything, some things are within your control. Wiseman writes, "What you can control is clearly communicating your beliefs about relationships. For example, how do you define dating? Going to a movie? Making out in someone's basement?"

Wiseman adds, "What probably matters the most to you is that your child develop healthy emotional and physical boundaries. But have you expressed what you want those boundaries to be? Bottom line, when teens 'date' they should also maintain strong relationships with friends and family."

Keep the lines of communication with your youngster open. Your kids do look up to you.

Keep your heart with all vigilance, for from it flow the springs of life. (Proverbs 4:23)

Help me, Jesus, as I guide my children in my role as a parent.

Times Change, Kids Don't

When Don Larkin marked five decades at Archbishop Stepinac High School in White Plains, New York, he thought back about all he had seen change: faculty, classrooms, technology.

But the kids, Larkin notes, don't change. "Basically, a kid is a kid, and he is looking for knowledge and how he will be able to develop," says the teacher, coach and activities coordinator. "That is what teaching and education are all about."

For Larkin, faith is part of the curriculum too. "The school helps strengthen the faith of the young people who come here, and if you are part of it, you also strengthen your own faith," he says.

Who are the young people in your life? How are you helping them learn—and learn to love their neighbor?

The glory of youths is their strength, but the beauty of the aged is their gray hair. (Proverbs 20:29)

I am Your child, Father; teach me Your ways.

Quick-Thinking Eighth-Grader Saves Lives

How would you feel if you saved the lives of both your best friend and your teacher in just one week? Eighth-grader Travon Avery had one such week, which began when he first prevented his best friend, Jose, from choking on a candy bar, using the Heimlich maneuver.

Later that week, the Chicago youth noticed his math teacher leaning heavily against the board in class. "We thought she was just sleeping," Avery told *Good Morning America*, "but she was passed out. I checked to see if she was breathing and she was, so I ran out of class and got the nurse."

Thanks to Avery's quick thinking, his teacher was taken to the hospital, where she was diagnosed with a severe migraine. Avery's heroic actions have since garnered him numerous accolades. In addition to winning a $10,000 scholarship, he was also named a Harvey's Hero on *The Steve Harvey Show*.

"My mom taught me if someone needed help not to just stand there and not do anything, but to make an effort and try," Avery declared. Beautiful words for us all to live by.

Do not forsake your friend. (Proverbs 27:10)

Jesus, may we never hesitate to reach out a hand to others.

From Drugs to Living Water

On November 2, 1967, singer Johnny Cash, who was struggling with drug abuse, was arrested in Lafayette, Georgia, for carrying amphetamines. Sheriff Ralph Jones showed Cash clemency, but asked him why he was willing to throw away his family and career for the sake of getting stoned. The singer later admitted that conversation was like a wake-up call from God.

As recounted in Steve Turner's book *The Man Called Cash,* the singer attended a service at First Baptist Church in Hendersonville, Tennessee, a few days later with future wife June Carter. In his sermon, Rev. Courtney Wilson spoke about the Samaritan woman Jesus met at the well to whom He told, "Whoever drinks the water I give him will never thirst."

Rev. Wilson remembered Cash's response: "Johnny later said that it made him determined that he was going to try that living water, that faith in Christ, instead of going the way he'd been going....From that time on his relationship with God, with Jesus Christ, was very real. He kept it current in his life."

The water that I will give will become in them a spring of water gushing up to eternal life. (John 4:14)

May Your living water cleanse and renew me, Jesus.

I Am Second

Nineteen-year-old *American Idol* winner Scotty McCreery is known for wearing a wristband that says "I Am Second." The purpose is to remind himself that God comes first in his life.

The Garner, North Carolina native first heard of the "I Am Second" movement in high school when his local church started feeding the football team dinner before games on Fridays. They'd eat while listening to a message from a community member, always with the theme "I Am Second." The players would then head to the game wearing their wristbands to remind them there was something bigger in life—even bigger than Friday night football in the South.

That reliance on his faith remained when McCreery competed on *American Idol.* Fame and the constant pressure to perform came hard and fast, but he had a way to deal with it. He said on *Christopher Closeup,* "Sometimes, I would Skype with my church group back home...and we all prayed together. Then I'd go do the show."

Wherever life takes you, stay focused on God.

I desire steadfast love. (Hosea 6:6)

Each day, Lord, increase my faith.

A Homeless Man Pays It Forward

In the Bible, Jesus praised the poor widow who put two copper coins in the treasury because she was giving out of her poverty, unlike the Pharisees who contributed only their excess money. That widow has a kindred spirit in Ed Denst, a 77-year-old homeless man in Los Angeles.

Living on the streets for more than 20 years, Denst receives a free meal every day when he goes to Our Mother of Good Counsel Church, which serves the local homeless population. As reported by *CBS LA*, that food comes from the St. Vincent de Paul Society's sandwich program.

As a longtime recipient of the kindness of others, Denst decided that he wanted to give back. He collected $250 through begging, and donated it to the Society of St. Vincent de Paul Council of Los Angeles. Board president Claire Padama said, "I think that's more meaningful than those people who have a lot."

Ed Denst adds, "What I'm learning is that people are charitable and that should make me thankful."

All of them have contributed out of their abundance, but she out of her poverty. (Luke 21:3-4)

May I extend my hand to others, Divine Savior.

The Gifts God Gave You

Christopher Award-winning author Nicole Lataif knew from an early age what school subjects she was good at—and which ones she struggled with. Thankfully, her parents saw where her gifts lay and encouraged her in that direction.

Lataif shared this story on the Pauline Kids website: "At the age of six, I stood up at a fundraiser in front of hundreds of people and read a poem I wrote encouraging people to give money to the poor. However, if you gave me a math problem, I froze. Numbers are not my thing! My parents never pressured me to crunch numbers as quickly as my math-savvy brother. They only encouraged me to do my best *with what God gave me*."

Lataif concluded, "Children will be happy and able to express love if you encourage them to do their best, not be someone they are not. As St. Thérèse stated, 'The splendor of the rose and the whiteness of the lily do not rob the little violet of its scent nor the daisy of its simple charm. If every tiny flower wanted to be a rose, spring would lose its loveliness.'"

Bless your maker who fills you with His good gifts. (Sirach 32:13)

Help me develop my unique potential, Loving Creator.

God at Harvard

As he recounts in his book *Fearing the Stigmata: Humorously Holy Stories of a Young Catholic's Search for a Culturally Relevant Faith,* Matt Weber grew up in an environment that was very supportive of his religious beliefs. Once he started attending Harvard University, however, no one was talking about faith there because it could be seen as somewhat anti-intellectual.

After he started bringing up his Catholicism on campus, Weber was shocked to discover that people of other faiths wanted to talk about their religious beliefs with him.

During an interview on *Christopher Closeup,* Weber said, "All of a sudden, I was meeting with students from the Jewish tradition, the Baha'i faith, a man who was Sikh, and atheists were picking my brain in really nice exchanges...At the beginning of my time there, I was afraid to be Catholic to some degree...At the end, we were hosting a Catholic Mass in one of the most prestigious classrooms at Harvard University...It was a joyous end to my experience there."

Be mutually encouraged by each other's faith. (Romans 1:12)

Increase my willingness to share my faith, Lord.

Survivors and Heroes

After more than a year, the effects of Superstorm Sandy still haunt some homeowners in the New York-New Jersey area.

Thankfully, David Wright, the gifted third baseman of the New York Mets, has been on the scene from the beginning and now heads The Wright Thing, a program to keep the plight of storm victims before the public.

Wright said, "New York is my second home…and so when I visited some of the neighborhoods that were destroyed by Sandy, my heart went out to these people."

Last summer Wright recognized two heroes of the storm: firefighter Tommy Woods of Queens, who helped evacuate stranded neighbors that night, and Elaine Wepa Gil, who entertained Staten Island youngsters and kept their mind off the storm. They not only got to meet Wright, but also received special honors at the Mets' Citi Field.

"We want to honor people like Tommy and Elaine," Wright said. "To say we haven't forgotten. Mostly I want to meet these heroes so I can have the chance to say, 'Thank you.'"

He is a man held in honor. (1 Samuel 9:6)

Help us recognize the heroes among us, Lord.

An Unknown Story of 9/11

When the Twin Towers collapsed during the 9/11 terror attacks, nearly 500,000 New Yorkers were stranded in lower Manhattan with no way out. Then the boats came to the rescue.

As reported by Katharine Herrup for *Reuters* and documented in the short film *Boatlift,* a distress call went out from the U.S. Coast Guard, resulting in every type of boat in the area—water taxis, tugboats, private boats, party boats—gathering to carry people to the other boroughs.

Herrup writes, "It was the ethic code of the seas that made the boat rescues such a success. If a boat needed refueling, another one would pull up alongside it and give it 10,000 gallons of fuel with no questions asked or no one asking for payment. If a woman in a wheelchair needed to be lifted over the fence on the water's edge to get into one of the boats, there were more than enough hands to help lift her...No one was left behind."

Within nine hours, half a million people had been ferried to safety because good people selflessly worked together.

God has granted safety to all those who are sailing with you. (Acts 27:24)

Let us work together to help each other, Savior.

Where is God in All of This?

Parents of children who suffer with serious medical conditions may ask, "Where is God in all of this?" Shelley Colquitt from the blog Confessions of a Sleep Deprived Momma offers an answer from her life.

Colquitt's daughter, whom she calls Mighty Z online, was born with a rare neurological disorder that seriously affects her breathing. Her medical troubles abound, yet Colquitt saw God's presence when she looked back through the years.

God was there, she writes, through a neonatologist who had seen a baby with Mighty Z's condition one month prior and therefore knew the one specialist who could help her. God was present through the doctor who helped wean Mighty Z off her ventilator during daytime hours. God was present when He led the family to a school and community that understands and supports them.

Colquitt concludes, "Our footsteps have been ordered by HIM every step of the way...When life has gotten too tough for us, He said, 'You are weak, I am strong.'"

He has pity on the weak and the needy. (Psalm 72:13)

Guide parents and children through all troubles, Father.

A Sister Takes a Chance

Sister Mary Rose McGeady, who died on September 13, 2012, came along at just the right moment to keep an important institution from falling flat on its face. A member of the Daughters of Charity of St. Vincent de Paul, she had spent a full career in child care when, in 1990, she came in for an interview to head Covenant House, then struggling to stay afloat.

The priest who had led the organization was mired in accusations of impropriety, and Covenant House, which gave new chances to youths in trouble, was in danger of toppling. Sister Mary Rose was 62 years old at the time.

Cardinal John O'Connor, who headed the selection committee, was dazzled by the interview; Sister Mary Rose was hired. By the time she retired 13 years later, Covenant House had opened new crisis centers and residential programs. Today, it serves more than 57,000 troubled youths in six countries.

Sister Mary Rose made it happen—one person who wasn't afraid to take a chance, and see what the Good Lord had in mind.

For surely I know the plans I have for you...to give you a future with hope. (Jeremiah 29:11)

God, may we trust in Your ability to work good in our lives.

Learning the Brain

Because the human brain is so complex and so unique to each person, a "one-size-fits-all" model for education just won't work, says psychologist Louis Cozolino.

So how's a teacher to teach? Cozolino suggests it's less about lesson plans and more about what makes the brain feel at home—and ready to learn.

For example, since the brain is a social organ, teachers should look for ways to create a caring classroom. And because mind and body are connected, physical activity—like playtime—should be part of the learning process.

Each one of us is also unique—"wonderfully made," as the Psalms tell us—known and loved by God. That's a fact to keep in mind each and every day.

Your hands have made and fashioned me; give me understanding that I may learn Your commandments. (Psalm 119:73)

I give You praise, Father, for You have put Your Spirit within me.

God Doesn't Look at Age

"Do you feel that God is asking you to do something else? Do you feel that you're too old?"

Those are the questions Barbara B. Etta asked herself 10 years ago after retiring from a long career of teaching and social work. Seventy years old at the time, she felt as if God was calling her to a life of ministry so she enrolled in Union Presbyterian Seminary in Richmond, Virginia.

Etta told the *Richmond Times-Dispatch*, "I came to the realization that God doesn't look at age. He doesn't look at race. He selects people to be by His side, to walk with Him, to talk with Him, to really help people in need. And that's what I had always been doing."

On May 25, 2013, at age 80, Etta graduated with a Master of Divinity degree. She acknowledges that God is "the final decision-maker" about her future, but hopes to use her skills to be of service. She said, "You see people...abusing their loved ones. And you also see a lot of killing. So the issue is, where are the people who are supposed to serve them? Are they there?"

**I am among you as one who serves.
(Luke 22:27)**

Help me be of service into a ripe old age, Father.

Terrible Towel, Great Legacy

In 1975, Pittsburgh Steelers radio announcer Myron Cope got the idea for the "Terrible Towel," the yellow, gold and black towels that fans wave at games to intimidate the opposing team. An official "Terrible Towel" was soon created, from which Cope received profits. But he didn't keep that money for himself.

In 1996, Cope signed over his "Terrible Towel" rights to the Allegheny Valley School, where his son Danny lived. Danny suffered from severe mental retardation since infancy so he found a home at the school which offers programs for children and adults with intellectual and developmental disabilities.

Because the towels are so popular, the school receives tens of thousands of dollars a month, which they use to buy special wheelchairs and other devices and programs.

Though Myron Cope died in 2008, his good work continues. Regis Champ, CEO of Allegheny Valley School, says, "Myron understood his mortality. The one thing that gave him great comfort was the knowledge that the legacy of the Terrible Towel would continue."

I have set you an example. (John 13:15)

Father, guide me in making selfless choices.

The Objects of Our Desire

Though we modern folk believe we're smarter and less gullible than, for example, the Israelites who lived thousands of years ago and built themselves a golden calf to worship, we are just as willing to bow down before false gods as they were.

Author Elizabeth Scalia, writing in her book *Strange Gods: Unmasking the Idols in Everyday Life,* explains why God made the first commandment, "I am the Lord, your God, you shall have no other gods besides Me."

She says, "All of the commandments are simply an expansion of the very first commandment…This command is given primacy not because the Creator is insecure and in constant need of attention, but because it is the one commandment that, if obeyed, renders all of the others nearly moot. Were we not continually making idols of the objects of our desire…nothing would be cluttering up the space between ourselves and God…The 'you shall nots' are less a list of restrictions than an invitation to keep turning back to God, who will 'satisfy the desire of every living thing.' (Psalm 145:16)"

Seek Me and live. (Amos 5:4)

Help me clear the clutter from my life, Lord.

A Prayer to Start the Day

Here's a prayer written by Cardinal John Henry Newman to start the day: "May all I do today begin with You, O Lord. Plant dreams and hopes within my soul, revive my tired spirit...

"May all I do today continue with Your help, O Lord. Be at my side and walk with me. Be my support today. May all I do today reach far and wide...My thoughts, my work, my life: make them blessings for Your kingdom; let them go beyond today.

"O God, Today is new unlike any other day, for God makes each day different. Today God's everyday grace falls on my soul like abundant seed, though I may hardly see it. Today is one of those days Jesus promised to be with me, a companion on my journey. And my life today, if I trust Him, has consequences unseen. My life has a purpose.

"I have a mission...I am a link in a chain, a bond of connection between persons. God has not created me for naught...Therefore I will trust Him. Whatever, wherever I am, I can never be thrown away. God does nothing in vain. He knows what He is about."

God...fulfills His purpose for me. (Psalm 57:2)

Help me make the most of each new day, Heavenly Father.

Special Angels Recreation

"Most kids...play football, have friends, go to the mall—things that our kids never get to do," said Deborah Wertalik of North Arlington, New Jersey. "We got tired of it. Our kids are great, and we want them to experience those things, too."

The "kids" Wertalik referred to, speaking for the other parents in her group, were young people with developmental disabilities like autism and Down syndrome. She did something about it, too, in a big way. First she organized Putting the Pieces Together, a support group for parents. Then she started Special Angels Recreation, which sponsored sporting events and movie trips for the youngsters.

Finally, there was the "Extreme Prom," with all of those developmentally disabled young people able to enjoy a prom night just as other kids in the U.S. do—with decorations, music and refreshments to boot. Stephanie Fritch of Montclair was thrilled for her 13-year-old son, Jackson, who has autism. "It's a big deal for him; it's a big deal for me," she said. "I never thought he'd get to experience this."

You shall not...put a stumbling block before the blind. (Leviticus 19:14)

Father, may we never alienate anyone for being different.

The Measure of Who We Are

Steve Gleason has lost the ability to make himself heard, but the words he posted on his Facebook page spoke volumes. The message was a simple one: "Received and accepted." With that an ugly chapter in the history of sports radio came to a close.

Gleason, a former member of the NFL New Orleans Saints, suffers from ALS (Lou Gehrig's disease), and he was responding to an apology— an apology from the same talk radio hosts who, incredibly, had mocked him and his illness. Why they hadn't chucked the whole idea before the words were aired remains a mystery, but Gleason was clearly above the fray.

"We have all made mistakes in this life," he added to the message he posted. "How we learn from our mistakes is the measure of who we are."

Gleason could have lashed back, but instead chose to forgive—and in the process showed the measure of who *he* is for everyone to see.

For the measure you give will be the measure you get back. (Luke 6:38)

Holy Redeemer, may we be as merciful and forgiving toward others as You are towards us.

Requiem for the Printer's Mass

The Printer's Mass at the downtown parish of St. Vincent de Paul in Baltimore is no more. When it began in 1914 (at 2:30 a.m.), many worshipers, reasonably enough, were printers.

Fresh from producing hefty Sunday editions, they packed the church to fulfill their sabbath obligation and, typically, went home. Over the years, though, some papers went out of business, others moved to the suburbs, and attendance at the Mass—now moved to 12:15 a.m.—gradually dwindled.

A story in the *Catholic Review* recalled some of the glory days of the Printer's Mass. The church's pastor, Father Richard Lawrence, remembered that as a collegian he would take a date out for a soda after a dance, then go with her to the Printer's Mass and slip a parish bulletin in his pocket. When an angry father wanted to know where his daughter could have been, the collegian turned pastor had a ready answer. "With the bulletin," he recalled, "you went from being the scoundrel of the world to a prospective son-in-law." Fond memories of a time gone by.

Let your heart cheer you in the days of your youth. (Ecclesiastes 11:9)

Jesus, may we cherish the carefree memories of our youth.

A Place of Brothers

Ever heard of the Bruderhof? The word means "place of brothers," and brotherhood is what Bruderhof is all about. Claudia McDonnell wrote about it in her column in *Catholic New York* last year, a column occasioned by the death of a personal friend who had been prominent in the movement.

Rooted in the Anabaptist tradition, the Bruderhof lives simply, opposes violence, and seeks to serve God and neighbor. It adheres to many early Christian teachings, especially those regarding marriage and sexuality, and is strongly pro-life. That helped to open up friendships and dialogue between the Bruderhof and the Catholic Church, particularly in the New York area under the guidance of the late Cardinal John O'Connor.

Bruderhof members actively engage in the Christian injunction to "love thy neighbor," O'Connell wrote. Explaining that's what all of us as Christians are expected to do, she specified: "Take care of each other, anticipate the other's needs, be there when help is needed, stay attentive."

Those who do not love a brother or sister they have seen, cannot love God whom they have not seen. (1 John 4:20)

May we remember we are all brothers and sisters, Lord.

Second Chances at 'Old Skool Café'

When she worked as a juvenile probation officer in San Francisco, Teresa Goines got to know a lot of teens whose lives were headed toward the dead end of crime. She wished someone could see that they were really just "boys" who could live a productive life with the right guidance.

After retiring from her job in 2005, Goines put all her retirement savings into opening Old Skool Café. Its motto is, "Come hungry, leave inspired." As reported by *ABC News,* Goines employs 11 young men and women with a criminal past as her cooks, dishwashers and service staff. If they abide by her strict rules, she offers them full-time jobs. Jeremiah, a 20-year-old with six prior arrests, used to rob people at gunpoint. After working at Old Skool Café, he doesn't want to return to his old ways. "That's a waste of life," he says.

Goines is satisfied with her work so far. She concludes, "When I look around, I see these young people are my investment and I couldn't imagine a better way to spend money. This is a dream come true."

To those who repent He grants a return. (Sirach 17:24)

Lord, help people in trouble turn their lives around.

The Way the World Is Meant to Work

When former Sandy Hook Elementary School teacher Kaitlin Roig heard gunshots in the school on Dec. 14, 2012, she immediately moved her 14 first-graders into a bathroom and blockaded the door, thereby saving them from the gunman. In the weeks following the carnage, the youngsters were overwhelmed by donations of gifts that came in from around the world.

During an interview on *Christopher Closeup*, Roig recalled telling her students, "In life, when somebody does something nice for you, you turn around and do something nice for someone else. That's the way the world is meant to work."

She decided that her class would find another class in the United States to whom they could send a gift. The excited reaction she got from her students prompted her to create the nonprofit Classes4Classes, which would encourage students around the country to provide gifts for less fortunate schools. The acts of kindness are documented on the website Classes4Classes.org.

If Kaitlin Roig and her students can create a little light out of the darkness they experienced, surely we can do the same.

Imitate what is good. (3 John 1:11)

Help me respond to evil with goodness, Lord.

The Last of the Human Freedoms

Though his high school science teacher in Vienna once declared, "Life is nothing more than a combustion process, a process of oxidation," Viktor Frankl always believed that life had meaning and purpose. He went on to become a renowned psychiatrist, a Jew who survived years of imprisonment in the Nazi concentration camp where his wife and parents perished.

Dr. Frankl served as a therapist to his fellow Jews and observed those who found meaning in their lives—even during horrific circumstances—had a better chance at survival. He once talked a man out of committing suicide by pointing out that he had a young child who needed him.

In his book *Man's Search for Meaning,* Dr. Frankl explained, "Everything can be taken from a man but one thing, the last of the human freedoms—to choose one's attitude in any given set of circumstances...A man who becomes conscious of the responsibility he bears toward a human being...will never be able to throw away his life. He knows the 'why' for his existence, and will be able to bear almost any 'how.'"

The Lord will fulfill His purpose for me. (Psalm 138:8)

Clarify Your purpose for my life, Divine Creator.

Rest and Refresh

According to experts, many people are sleep-deprived which is detrimental to their health and a potential danger to others. Drivers who doze at the wheel and workers who fall asleep on the job, for instance, put others at risk.

In its May 2013 issue, *Consumer Reports* magazine offered tips to help you get more zzzs.

- Keep a consistent schedule. Don't vary bedtime and wake-up time by more than an hour, even on weekends.
- Exercise—but not too late. Leave time to unwind.
- Curb late-night snacking.
- Wean yourself off sleep meds; use only occasionally.
- Adjust your temperature. Hot shower and cool bedroom.
- Lay off the sauce. Alcohol can disrupt sleep.
- Turn off the tube. No TV, computer, smartphone.
- Decaffeinate your evenings. Avoid coffee, colas and other foods with caffeine.

Return, O my soul, to your rest, for the Lord has dealt bountifully with you. (Psalm 116:7)

Holy Spirit, guide and comfort us.

Interfaith Counsel and Comfort

South Florida's Catholic Hospice, which is associated with Holy Cross Hospital in Fort Lauderdale, has been providing physical and spiritual end-of-life care to Jewish residents for several years. Now they plan to expand the program by opening two new facilities and hiring several rabbis.

As reported in *The Sun Sentinel*, the L'Chaim Jewish Hospice program was created in 2003 as part of Catholic Hospice. All non-Jewish workers are trained in the customs and traditions of Judaism in order to be respectful of patients' needs.

Rabbi Ira Eisenmann provides "counsel, comfort and advice" to patients and their families to help ease their burdens during this trying time. He praises the Catholic-Jewish connection that has been forged through the hospice ministry: "They were very respectful of me from the first day I stepped in the door...Our relations couldn't be better. Catholic Hospice itself is a family. We're all working together toward one goal—the best possible treatment of our patients and their families."

How very good and pleasant it is when kindred live together in unity! (Psalm 133:1)

Foster a spirit of cooperation among all peoples, Creator.

A Broadcaster's Personal Cause

Chris Carrino is best known as the radio voice of the Brooklyn Nets, but to a growing number of fans he's also head of a foundation that raises funds to fight a form of muscular dystrophy (MD). He knows all about the ailment, too; he was diagnosed with it during his college years.

"Maybe it was time for me to come forward and do something that could have an impact," he said, although in the past he was reluctant to talk about it. Now he's launched the Chris Carrino Foundation for FSHD. The initials are shorthand for facioscapulohumeral dystrophy, one of nine types of MD. FSHD usually strikes young adults by the time they're 20, and affects the voluntary muscles in the face, shoulder and upper arms. There's no treatment for the disease, nor is there a cure.

So the 42-year-old Carrino has a dual focus these days: NBA basketball with the Nets, and life with a form of MD. "I want to be an example for kids who are going to be diagnosed," he said, "and who don't know that the dreams they had can still be accomplished."

Let your heart take courage. (Psalm 27:14)

Jesus, help us to see possibility instead of negativity when faced with illness.

The Iron Lady's WWII Kindness

Margaret Thatcher, who died in 2013, left a legacy of many great accomplishments on the world stage. She became the first woman to be elected British prime minister, and her work helped bring an end to the Soviet Union. Yet Thatcher often named her greatest accomplishment as being her role in helping to save a Jewish teenager from Nazi terror in Austria.

According to Charles Johnson's report on Thatcher's relationships with Jews, the future prime minister's older sister, Muriel, received a letter in 1938 from her pen pal in Austria, 17-year-old Edith Muhlbauer. Edith informed Muriel that the Nazis were rounding up Jews, and she feared she might be next. Could Muriel's family help her escape from Austria, she asked.

Muriel and Margaret raised money with the help of a local Rotary Club to get Edith out. They accomplished their task, bringing Edith to England, where she stayed with many Rotary families for the next two years before joining relatives in South America. The lesson, explained Thatcher in 1995: "Never hesitate to do whatever you can, for you may save a life."

You have saved us from our foes. (Psalm 44:7)

Grant me courage to help the persecuted, Lord.

Good Leaders, Weak Leaders

On his website LifeSupportSystem.com, Steve Goodier differentiates between good and weak leaders:

- Good leaders size up the situation, put themselves in the right position to respond, prepare, and then act at the proper time. Weak leaders are blind to the current situation.

- Good leaders encourage. They give credit when things go well and take responsibility when they don't. Weak leaders discourage others. They find fault and blame.

- Good leaders are perpetual learners. Weak leaders know it all. They already have the answers.

- Good leaders will often go where there is no path and leave a trail. Weak leaders prefer to keep things as they are, even if the system is not working all that well.

- Good leaders help their subordinates find success. They realize that when one is lifted to another's shoulders, both stand taller. Weak leaders sabotage the successes of others. When those below them succeed, they feel threatened.

Receive a wreath for your excellent leadership. (Sirach 32:2)

Help me to be a servant leader like You, Jesus.

Serving God in Possible Things

During the era when St. Thérèse of Lisieux served as a Carmelite nun, France passed laws restricting religious orders. Her sister, Celine, also a nun, was consumed by anger about this. Thérèse told her not to be concerned about such matters because they had no power over them. "Our only duty," she explained, "is to become united to God."

Writing in *The Love That Keeps Us Sane: Living the Little Way of St. Thérèse of Lisieux,* author Marc Foley, O.C.D. asks, "What could a cloistered nun in 19th-century France do about the political situation except pray and be faithful to her vocation?"

He then cites the words of St. Teresa of Avila, whose insights could apply to Celine—or any of us living with anxiety today: "Sometimes the devil gives us great desires so that we will avoid setting ourselves to the task at hand, serving our Lord in possible things, and instead be content with having desired the impossible."

Work with God to achieve the possible.

Cast all your anxiety on Him, because He cares for you. (1 Peter 5:7)

Father, help me serve You with peace of mind and heart.

A Surprising Touchdown

Despite being confined to a wheelchair due to cerebral palsy, 13-year-old Jack McGraw from Haines Middle School in St. Charles, Illinois, has been part of the school's football team for two years. Coach Sean Masoncup notes the young sports lover is on the sidelines for every game, offering moral support.

Coach Masoncup started the 2012 season with the goal of having Jack score a touchdown, holding the football in one hand while driving his motorized wheelchair with the other. That happened during the Football Invitational Tournament, and came as a big surprise to Jack.

As reported by *ABC News,* the opposing team took a knee during the final play of the game, gave Jack possession of the ball, and allowed him to make his way to the end zone. Parents, team members and even opposing players cheered him on.

Coach Masoncup said, "I think he was a little nervous, but once he scored, he was just ecstatic. It was one of the best moments of my coaching career."

For God all things are possible. (Mark 10:27)

Instill young people and their coaches with genuine sportsmanship, Lord.

An Actress's Motivation

For her role as Fantine in the Christopher Award-winning movie *Les Misérables*, Anne Hathaway approached the character from a place of pain. Fantine, you see, is a mother forced to work as a prostitute in order to financially support her daughter.

Hathaway didn't just consider her as a character in 19th-century France, but as one of the real women today who are victims of sexual slavery. She researched the topic, and one story she saw stayed with her.

Hathaway said, "This woman kept repeating, 'I come from a good family. We lost everything and I have children. So now I do this.' She didn't want to do this, but it was the only way her children were going to eat. Then she let out this sob like I've never heard before. And she raised her hand to her forehead, and it was the most despairing gesture I've ever seen. That was the moment I realized I wasn't [just] playing a character; this woman deserves to have her voice heard."

Do not let the downtrodden be put to shame; let the poor and needy praise Your name. (Psalm 74:21)

Rescue those trapped in sexual slavery, Divine Savior.

Winton's Children

In 1939, 29-year-old stockbroker Nicholas Winton opted to visit a friend in Prague rather than go on a ski vacation. Once there, he saw how dangerous life was for the young Jewish refugees forced to flee the Nazi-dominated Sudetenland.

Many countries had organizations to help Jewish children escape to a safe haven, but Prague had none. So Winton took it upon himself to find countries that would shelter them. Britain and Sweden agreed, and Winton saved 669 Jewish lives.

Not until nearly 50 years later, when Winton's wife found the records detailing his brave act, were his rescue efforts revealed. At his wife's urging, Winton agreed to appear on a *BBC* show called *That's Life* to share his tale. Many of the children he rescued were seated in the audience. He corresponds with them to this day, and although many are grandparents now, they will forever consider themselves "Winton's Children."

"Don't be content...just to do no wrong," Winton told a history class. "Be prepared every day to try to do some good."

So let us not grow weary in doing what is right. (Galatians 6:9)

Jesus, bless all good deeds, known and unknown.

A Short But Meaningful Life

Katyia Rowe and Shane Johnson from Shropshire, England, received a devastating diagnosis from doctors about their unborn son: his brain wasn't forming properly so he would never be able to walk or talk, and he would likely need round-the-clock care his entire life.

Doctors offered to terminate the pregnancy at 24 weeks. Rowe and Johnson considered the idea until a 3D sonogram showed the boy in the womb smiling and waving his arms.

Rowe told *The Daily Mail,* "Despite all the awful things I was being told, while he was inside me his quality of life looked to be wonderful...I was told he would never walk or talk yet the scans showed him constantly wriggling and moving. As I watched I knew that...it was my duty as a mother to protect [him]. No matter how long he had left, he deserved to live."

Tragically, the child, who his parents named Lucian, died nine hours after being born. Rowe still relishes her time with him: "The love and joy I felt the moment I put Lucian in my arms told me it had all been worth it."

Let her who bore you rejoice. (Proverbs 23:25)

Instill in us a respect for all life, Savior.

Pursuing Truth

"Truth is its own witness," is an old Jewish saying. In a similar vein, an Arab proverb provides this reminder: "He who has the truth is in the majority, even though he be one."

Down through the centuries, people of every nation have paid tribute to truth. If you're not familiar with them, reflect prayerfully on some of these proverbs:

- "To withhold truth is to bury gold." (Danish)
- "It takes a great many shovels full to bury the truth." (German)
- "Truth will get out, even if buried in a gold coffin." (Russian)

A reverence for truth has been planted in the heart of every human being by the Creator. It is so deeply imbedded that it can never be completely ignored or rooted out.

Strengthen and develop the sense of truth within you, and you will become a more effective Christopher—or Christ-bearer—in our world.

I am the way, and the truth, and the life. (John 14:6)

Increase in us, Divine Savior, a love of truth.

Unity on the Roof

When members of North Carolina's Rutherfordton First Baptist church volunteered to roof a house for a charity event in 2002, the only congregants who showed up were three women. Even though they had no experience, veteran roofer Rev. Billy Honeycutt put them all to work. And so was born the Women Roofers of Rutherford County.

As reported by *CBS News*, they only help people with a low median income. And they've become such roofing pros that they no longer need a professional male overseer.

Their number has long grown beyond church members, and includes a nurse, a pharmacist, small business owners, and retirees who simply want to help the less fortunate while having some fun.

Nell Bovender, the Women Roofers' leader, adds, "Take a lesson from what we do because I work alongside this group of women—some of the most conservative Republicans, some of the most liberal Democrats—and we're working together for a common good."

Be united in...the same purpose. (1 Corinthians 1:10)

Holy Spirit, unite us in accomplishing God's good will.

In Sickness and In Health

When both he and his wife were suffering from nasty winter colds at the same time in 2013, Patheos.com blogger Thomas McDonald grew reflective about the "in sickness and in health" part of their marriage vows. He regretted that he wasn't able to serve his wife better during her time of need.

Though service and sacrifice are sometimes seen as getting in the way of happiness and personal fulfillment in today's world, they are really the sources of true joy, according to McDonald. He writes, "We are all broken, fallen people, but I'm a bit more broken than most. My wife found me, picked me up, healed me, and gave me the other half of her soul. How can a gift that sacred and beautiful not produce joy?"

McDonald concludes, "My wife and I have had more good days than bad…But love is light, and light casts shadows; those shadows are sickness, sadness and death. All things will fade: health, beauty, strength. When we are stripped of it all before the face of God, only the love will remain. And that love will be light, and that light will be eternal."

The light of the righteous rejoices. (Proverbs 13:9)

Give married couples the strength to endure trials, Father.

Little Miracles

The New York Life Center in Brooklyn, New York, is a non-sectarian facility for pregnant women and young mothers. Though it's run by Catholics, the center helps women of all faiths by offering them material, emotional and spiritual support both before and after their children are born.

The diversity of people helped at the center offers a vivid reminder of why our society needs more places like this. Writing in *The Tablet,* the diocesan newspaper for the Diocese of Brooklyn, editor-in-chief Ed Wilkinson notes that a Hispanic woman who doesn't speak English and a Muslim woman dressed in Arab garb both come into the center while he's there.

The Hispanic woman asks a worker if they have a size four jacket for her son. The Muslim woman, on the other hand, is returning clothes she had gotten for her daughter, who has outgrown them. She explains that she likely would have aborted her daughter if it wasn't for the Center's loving support.

Laura Sica, the office manager, adds, "There are a lot of little miracles that happen here."

Choose life. (Deuteronomy 30:19)

Move citizens and governments to respect life, Lord.

A Coach's Great Rewards

Coach Tom Coughlin led the New York Giants to Super Bowl victories in 2008 and 2012, making him the oldest coach to win a Super Bowl. He credits much of his on and off-the-field success to the values he learned from his parents and in Catholic school.

As Coughlin told *St. Anthony Messenger* magazine, his faith when working is not so much expressed in overtly religious ways, but in the focus he puts on the preparedness of his players, and the concern he shows for them as individuals.

Coughlin said, "At this stage of my career, the great rewards are to have players come back and tell you how much they appreciated what you believed in and how you taught them. And also for them to say to you, quite frankly, 'I love you.'...To use the actual phrase, 'I love you.' That's an incredible, emotional experience. Quite frankly, I don't know that you're prepared for it. It's the ultimate compliment. I appreciate that tremendously."

Teach them the good way in which they should walk. (1 Kings 8:36)

May my life be grounded in a love for You, Lord.

A Christopher Prayer for Doctors

Maryknoll Father James Keller, the founder of The Christophers, was once asked to prepare a prayer for doctors by the Abbott Laboratories of Chicago. This is what he wrote:

"Thank you, O Lord, for the privilege of being a doctor; for letting me serve as Your instrument in ministering to the sick and afflicted. May I always treat with reverence the human life which You have brought into being. Keep me constantly alert to see that the sacred right to live is never violated for even the least individual. Deepen my love for people so that I will always give of myself gladly and generously to those stricken with illness.

"Help me to listen patiently, diagnose carefully, prescribe conscientiously, and follow through faithfully...Let me be calm without being cold, patient without being weak, and strong without being proud. Help me Lord, to give encouragement without overconfidence...May I be prompt to relieve pain, quick to hold out the hand of honest hope. Inspire me always to show a special tenderness for the poor and forgotten, for those who are broken in spirit as well as in body. Amen."

**Honor physicians for their services.
(Sirach 38:1)**

Lord, endow doctors with competence and compassion.

Entering the Story of Faith

Amy Andrews, co-author of the book *Love and Salt: A Spiritual Friendship Shared in Letters,* grew up with an agnostic mother and atheist father, yet she'd always felt naturally drawn to God. As a writer interested in literature, it was her desire to enter into the "story" of Christianity that eventually led her to the Catholic Church.

During an interview on *Christopher Closeup,* Andrews explained, "[Since I'd gotten married], I realized that you can't know something 100 percent ahead of time. You have to do it. Then you have the transformation and knowledge that come from actually being married. With that example, I started to think about faith in the same way—that this was not a matter of knowing everything ahead of time; it was a matter of entering a story. And the story had become so beautiful and so true and so desirable to me that I thought, 'This is as much as I'm going to be able to know from the outside. What I need to do now is enter the story and see what happens.'"

Be a part of God's story for you.

Press on to know the Lord. (Hosea 6:3)

Guide me along Your paths, O Lord.

Eclipse of the Moon

On Christopher Columbus' last journey to the Americas, he almost didn't make it to what is now Jamaica; his two ships were barely seaworthy because of damage done by shipworms.

At first, the island's inhabitants, Columbus and his companions got along well. But as weeks went by, the relationship became strained, and the natives stopped providing food and supplies.

Armed with his knowledge of an impending lunar eclipse, Columbus told the natives that if they didn't resume their help, the "gods" would take the moon from the sky. First derisive, the natives soon became frightened as the moon turned a blood red color, and slowly began to disappear. The island's inhabitants promised to renew their help if the moon would be "put back." It was, of course, at the end of the eclipse, and Columbus and his men were safe until rescue ships arrived some months later.

Our Lord Who sees all we do seeks always that we reach out in love to our neighbor.

Put away the foreign gods that are among you. (Genesis 35:2)

I sought Your help, Father, and You rescued me.

Tackling Technology Safety With Faith

Catholic and Greek Orthodox Christian parents alike have recently united to create a website that will better acquaint them with the Internet. According to Mark Pattison of *Catholic News Service*, this collaborative site's main purpose is "to instruct users, primarily parents, on how young people can navigate the online world."

The idea for such a website was first born at a Religious Alliance Against Pornography summit meeting two years ago.

"We were challenged to come up with actionable items as a result of the summit," Theo Nicolakis, chief information officer for the Greek Orthodox Church explains. "One of the items [was an] initiative that would give the voice of faith in regard to online safety."

Secretary of Communications for U.S. Bishops Helen Osman adds, "[The website] focuses a lot on helping them understand this world where their kids are more comfortable, to help the children understand the potential and also the risk."

The website is www.faithandsafety.org. Log on today!

Train children in the right way. (Proverbs 22:6)

Lord, guide children through today's technological world.

Feminine, Faithful, Free and Bold

As a spiritually restless college student, author and *EWTN* host Colleen Carroll Campbell didn't think that the saints could be relevant to her modern life and struggles. Then she discovered that St. Teresa of Avila was once a party girl who enjoyed male admirers, romance novels and fashion.

After an adolescent illness, Teresa wound up in a Carmelite convent where she engaged in a decades-long tug-of-war between her love of God and love of the world. When she finally confronted the superficiality and shallowness inside herself, she abandoned her worldly desires to focus fully on God. Teresa founded the Discalced Carmelites and reformed numerous convents. She is now a Doctor of the Church.

So what drew Campbell to her? During an interview on *Christopher Closeup* to discuss her Christopher Award-winning book *My Sisters the Saints,* she said, "Teresa directed all of her passion, vitality and joy toward God and His purposes...When I saw that a woman could be feminine and faithful, yet free and bold, I was inspired."

**The righteous are as bold as a lion.
(Proverbs 28:1)**

Give me the courage to follow You always, Lord Jesus.

An Alcoholic Fights His Demons

Country music legend George Jones, who died in 2013, lived a hard-partying life filled with alcohol and cocaine for much of his career. When he was interviewed on *The 700 Club* in 2003, he was asked about this dark period. Jones said, "You forget even that God exists or anybody does. My first wives or family or any of those things didn't matter anymore."

Jones was married four times, most famously to fellow country singer Tammy Wynette. His demons, however, kept him from a stable life until his fourth wife, Nancy, used some old-time religion to help him stop drinking.

Jones said, "The doctor told me that I wouldn't last another two months if things didn't change. I went to the hospital, and Nancy was there by my side. I went through 30 days of reading the Bible. The Bible was one of the books that I really believed in, but never lived or read like I should have. I didn't know there was a way back. But then I found that way back with the Lord's help and Nancy staying by my side."

Convince, rebuke and encourage with the utmost patience in teaching. (2 Timothy 4:2)

Heal my afflictions and addictions, Divine Physician.

Crossing the Finish Line

Eleven-year-old Ben Baltz knew he was in trouble when he felt his prosthetic leg coming loose during a triathlon on Pensacola Beach, Florida. It happened about a half-mile into his run, causing Baltz—who had lost his leg to bone cancer at age six—to fall down.

Determined to finish the race, he lay on the ground deciding whether he should hop or crawl the rest of the way. As reported by the *News Herald*, that's when Matthew Morgan, a Marine volunteer at the event, stepped in. Morgan asked Baltz if he needed help. When the boy responded, "Sure," Morgan picked him up and carried him. Baltz held onto Morgan with one hand, and his prosthetic leg with the other.

An announcer informed the crowd about what happened, so anticipation grew for the big finish. John Murray, one of the triathlon's organizers, recalled that when Baltz and Morgan crossed the finish line, "There wasn't a dry eye in the place."

One human being came to the aid of another human being in trouble. That's the way life should be every day.

Relieve the troubles of my heart. (Psalm 25:17)

May I extend my hand to others, Compassionate Father.

'He Would Rescue Me from Grief'

When the son of *Fox News* political analyst Brit Hume committed suicide in 1998, the newsman felt devastated. Though he'd called himself a Christian all his life, he admitted to never having given much thought to God in general. Following the suicide, however, Hume's heartbreak was intermingled with a memorable spiritual experience.

He told journalist David Brody, "I had the feeling through it all, that God was there, that He would rescue me from grief and pain, and that I would get through it, and I knew I believed, and I knew it with enormous force."

The public's reaction to Hume's loss eased his burden even further. He said, "My home address isn't well-known, and yet somehow, in the weeks that followed that incident of his death, we [sent] out 'thank you' notes to nearly a thousand people who had written to me...I was astonished at that response. I thought I was seeing the face of God. And I felt enormously lifted by it."

If you know someone enduring the loss of a loved one, be the face of God to them.

God, the Lord, is my strength. (Habakkuk 3:19)

Make Your presence known to the grieving, Savior.

The Bible Geek's Advice

Known as "The Bible Geek," Mark Hart works with the program Life Teen to help young people "form their Catholic identity in authentic and joy-filled ways."

How does he do that in an era when young people seem to be turning away from religion? Hart explained on *Christopher Closeup*, "Modern teenagers...want deep relationships; they just don't know how to have them. They're really drawn to the mystical. When you start walking them into the mystical elements of the sacraments and the depth and breadth of the mysteries of the church, their hearts become enlivened."

Hart sees part of the problem in reaching youth to be adults who talk at them, not to them. He points out, "We should take a lesson from Christ on the road to Emmaus. He walked and listened before He taught."

Despite the challenges of reaching teens, Hart concludes, "People talk about all the negatives of teenagers (but)...I am consistently amazed and blown away by the quality of our young people."

Train children in the right way. (Proverbs 22:6)

Give me the grace to talk with, not at, people, Father.

The First Thing They Need is Love

Jeanette Meyer has come full circle. The 63-year-old Minnesota woman was forced into early abortions by a controlling boyfriend years ago in New York, and returned to her Midwest roots to begin the healing process. It continued with her marriage, the birth of her five children, and culminated finally in 2005 in a Rachel's Vineyard weekend retreat, which included a healing service for all the post-abortive women taking part.

Two years ago she heard of an opening in a pregnancy center, applied for the job, and soon found herself as executive director of Pregnancy Choices in Apple Valley, Minnesota. Women come there from all walks of life, and counseling them can take a variety of turns.

Meyer relies heavily on her faith and the example of Jesus in living out her mission. But the women themselves, and the options they want to know about, are never far from her mind. "The first thing they need," she said, "is love."

And in Jeanette Meyer, they can find it without end.

Love one another deeply. (1 Peter 1:22)

Father, may love of humankind shape all our actions.

The Power of Family

In her book *No Greater Love,* Mother Teresa recalled finding a poverty-stricken little girl on the street in Calcutta, and taking her to the Missionaries of Charity's children's home where they provided her with food and clothes. The little girl remained there for a few hours, then ran away. A few days later, Mother Teresa found her again and brought her back—but this time she instructed one of the nuns to follow the girl when she left. The nun did so and found she went to her mother, who was living under a tree in the street, where she did her cooking.

Mother Teresa wrote, "I went there [and] asked the little girl, 'How is it that you would not stay with us?' She answered, 'I could not live without my mother. She loves me.' That little girl was happier to have the meager food her mother was cooking...than all the things I had given her. While the child was with us, I could scarcely see a smile on her face. But when I found her there with her mother, in the street, they were smiling. Why? Because they were family."

Appreciate the fulfilling love and power of family.

Love the family of believers. (1 Peter 2:17)

Father, strengthen the bonds within my family.

A Grad of Monkey College

The graduates of Monkey College are helping people with spinal cord injuries and mobility impairments live more independent and fulfilling lives. And yes, these graduates are actually monkeys: Capuchins, to be exact, because they're small, smart and naturally inclined to use tools.

As reported in *Parade,* a Boston-based non-profit called Helping Hands raises and trains these monkeys to be of service to individuals like Ned Sullivan, age 30, who became paralyzed after a car accident. His helper monkey, named Kasey, performs tasks that require motor skills, like turning on lights, opening cans, and loading DVDs. Sullivan also cares for Kasey to whatever degree he's able, giving him a sense of purpose.

Megan Talpert, executive director of Helping Hands, says, "We hear it time and time again from our recipients: 'I've got to get out of bed to take care of the monkey.' They have to think about needs outside of their own and that's really empowering."

Which of your responsibilities can be considered blessings?

Let each of you look not to your own interests, but to the interests of others. (Philippians 2:4)

Help me be of service to someone else, Holy Spirit.

How a Five-Year-Old Spent $20

Like most five-year-olds, Joshua Williams considered the fun things he could buy when his grandmother gave him a $20 bill. But while driving to church with his mother, he noticed a homeless beggar on the street. He asked her if she would stop the car so he could give the man his money to buy food.

That incident lit a spark in Joshua so his family soon began making meals to hand out to the local homeless population in Miami. The youngster still wanted to do more, however, so in 2007, when Joshua was seven, he and his mother established the Joshua's Heart Foundation. As reported in *Parade,* they've donated 400,000 pounds of food to the needy in a variety of ways, including a program that gives backpacks filled with food to hungry schoolchildren. Joshua says, "When kids don't have to worry whether they'll have dinner that night, they can concentrate better, do better in school."

And what does Joshua get from all his hard work? "When I look at the faces of the people we're helping and see how happy they are, that's my favorite moment."

**A generous person will be enriched.
(Proverbs 11:25)**

Nourish our bodies and our souls, Bountiful Lord.

The Acorn Planter

In his book *The Sower's Seeds: 120 Inspiring Stories for Preaching, Teaching and Public Speaking,* Father Brian Cavanaugh shares a story originally written by Jean Giono.

A young traveler exploring the French Alps during the 1930s came across a barren stretch of land that had been devastated by World War I. He was surprised to find an old man there carrying a sack of acorns and a four-foot pipe. The man poked holes in the ground with the pipe, then dropped in acorns.

The old man, named Elzeard Bouffier, had endured the death of his wife and son. He told the traveler, "I've planted over 100,000 acorns. Perhaps only a tenth of them will grow. [But] I want to do something useful."

Over two decades later, that same traveler returned to the desolate area where he had met the old man. He was shocked to see the land covered with "a forest two miles wide and five miles long. Birds were singing, animals were playing and wildflowers perfumed the air...all because someone cared."

**Prosper for us the work of our hands.
(Psalm 90:17)**

Use me as an instrument to build up Your creation, Heavenly Father.

Are Pancakes the Secret to Happiness?

Nataly Kogan bought into a certain perception of the American dream. Having arrived in the United States with her family at age 13 after escaping religious persecution in the Soviet Union, she believed she would eventually find happiness by building a successful career and earning lots of money.

Kogan chased that definition of happiness for 20 years, and accomplished some of what she wanted. Yet she felt exhausted and lacked fulfillment. Then she experienced an awakening.

As Kogan revealed in her talk at a TED Conference, which highlights "ideas worth spreading," she realized that pursuing the "big happy" was doomed to failure. Instead, it was the "small, tiny, positive moments" in life that were the true foundation of happiness—moments like the joy she experienced from making her young daughter a smiley-faced pancake for breakfast.

That revelation led Kogan to create Happier, Inc., which encourages people to stop saying "I'll be happier when…"—and to start saying "I'm happier now because…"

Appreciate the little joys in your life today.

**Happy are those who find wisdom.
(Proverbs 3:13)**

Holy Spirit, help me to choose happiness today.

A Life Changed by Understanding

Shannon Hageman's life changed forever after hearing the words, "I understand," from Father Jerel Scholl. In a Letter to the Editor of *Catholic Digest*, the Yutan, Nebraska woman explained, "Those were the words Father Jerel used in response to my excuses for my rare attendance at Mass...That's exactly what I needed to hear. I needed a spiritual father who understood. From the first time I heard his homily, the wall I'd put up between myself and the Church slowly began to crumble.

"Father Scholl and I crossed paths at a pivotal point in my life. I'd experienced great loss and I found myself in a hopeless pit of despair. Somehow, I knew my happiness depended on loving a God I felt so unloved by.

"My attendance at Mass slowly improved. For the first time, I was perceptive of homilies, more aware of the liturgy, and stumbling into prayerful conversations with Christ...I didn't know how to love God, and with Father Scholl, I learned that you cannot love someone you do not know. Father Scholl taught me to know God. Nothing can change a life quite like that."

**The Lord...understands every plan.
(1 Chronicles 28:9)**

May our spiritual parents guide us to You, Lord.

God's Finger on a Man's Shoulder

Maryknoll Father James Keller, the founder of The Christophers, once wrote the following words about bringing Christ's peace into the world:

"Someone once said, 'There is no surprise more magical than the surprise of being loved. It is God's finger on a man's shoulder.'

"If you love, you will be loved. You will also be living your religion, not just talking about it. And you will find developing within yourself an inner power that you little realized you possessed. The more you use it, the more it will grow. Life will take on new meaning. You will become more approachable. And you will understand why all people want to be truly loved, not just tolerated.

"Yes, you personally and individually can take Christ's peace into your own heart and home, so that it will radiate from there to every part of the world."

Peace I leave with you; My peace I give to you. I do not give to you as the world gives. Do not let your hearts be troubled, and do not let them be afraid. (John 14:27)

Teach me to live and share Your peace, Jesus.

Searching for a Cure

In the 25 years that Rick and Erica Kaitz of Boston volunteered to raise money for cancer research, they never envisioned the way in which their efforts would take a personal turn. But in June 2012, Erica was diagnosed with a rare form of uterine cancer, a sarcoma, called LMS. Because only 150 patients in the United States suffer with that particular form of cancer, there is little research or treatment available.

As reported by *ABC News*, Rick has now taken a leave of absence from his job to both care for his wife and try to find a cure for her. He organized a team of cyclists and runners for a race that will raise $1.5 million for research on these sarcomas.

In association with the Dana Farber Cancer Institute and Dr. George Demetri, who was instrumental in the advancement of the medicine Gleevec as a targeted cancer therapy, Rick hopes to make small but significant strides toward a treatment. He knows the road ahead will be difficult, but he'll do whatever he can for the woman he loves.

Let us hold fast to the confession of our hope. (Hebrews 10:23)

Help make the impossible possible, Lord of Life.

A Cut for St. Baldrick's

Many young women spend time making their hair look beautiful, but Joan Renee Cloutier did something beautiful by cutting all her hair off. She did it to support the St. Baldrick's Foundation, which raises money for childhood cancer research.

Cloutier, a 2010 graduate of St. John's University in Queens, New York, secured $5,800 in donations from family and friends for agreeing to shave her head in solidarity with childhood cancer patients. She returned to campus in 2013, where the official haircut took place.

That kind of selflessness is par for the course for this alumna who spent her college career taking part in on-campus service opportunities, a pilgrimage to Lourdes, France, and a mission trip to Panama, which she describes as "transformative."

Currently studying for her Clinical Doctorate in Audiology, which will qualify her to treat people with hearing disorders, Cloutier remains committed to serving others professionally and personally—and she credits St. John's with nurturing her development as "a Christian leader."

Serve God faithfully. (Tobit 14:8)

Inspire me to serve others joyfully, Holy Spirit.

Music, Poetry and the Sons of Santa

The Sons of Santa. That's the name 16-year-old Ben Walther and his friends chose for their cover band when they were in high school. In retrospect, the singer-songwriter and music minister now admits, "We were awful, but we thought we were rock stars." Yet, God can use any circumstance to draw people closer to Him, which is what happened to Walther.

During an interview on *Christopher Closeup*, he recalled that several members of the band, including himself, were feeling called by Christ to move more deeply into their faith. After performing an original song at a retreat, several girls approached them in tears and said, "That song reminded us so much of our good friend that we lost in a car accident two weeks ago." The girls then hugged them and left.

Ben said, "We realized at that moment just how powerful music ministry can be, when we take poetry and give it a melody. That was the birth of my vocation. I realized I want to do this for the rest of my life, to channel these gifts for God's glory because I saw how powerful it was for good."

Give glory to the Lord. (Joshua 7:19)

May my gifts glorify You, Divine Savior.

Outshining Your Fears

While lying in bed one night, irrational anxieties and fears started flooding writer Mary DeTurris Poust's thoughts. She reflected on how the pervasion of complete darkness, whether literal or figurative, can haunt us from adolescence to adulthood.

"What is it about darkness that makes normal things seem a little scarier?" DeTurris Poust muses in *Catholic New York*. "Maybe it has something to do with childhood memories of things that go bump in the night...Maybe it has something to do with the deep connection we make between darkness and evil in our faith and in our world."

Whatever the sources of our fears of the unseen, DeTurris Poust offers a powerful solution that will shed light into even the darkest corners of our existence.

"It might not happen in a day or week or even a month," she concludes, "but little by little when we return to prayer...the slant of light in the hallway of our minds grows bigger and brighter until there's no place left for fear and anxiety to hide."

He has redeemed my soul...my life shall see the light. (Job 33:28)

Father, may we take comfort in the light of Your presence.

The Greatest Ending in Movie History

The film *Les Miserables,* adapted from the popular Broadway musical, won a 2012 Christopher Award. It may also include the greatest ending in movie history. Why? Because it's the ending to which we all aspire.

The main character, Jean Valjean, endured great hardship in his life and was on a dead-end road before a Christ-like bishop provided him with mercy and a second chance. He came to accept responsibility not just for his own life, but the lives of those he grew to love: primarily, his adoptive daughter, Cosette. Valjean was indirectly responsible for the death of her mother, Fantine, and took in her little girl, from whom he learns selflessness.

When Valjean dies, his passing isn't depressing; it's celebratory! He is led into heaven by the bishop who showed him mercy—and by Fantine to whom he showed compassion.

Les Miserables beautifully reflects the reunion that will happen if we lead our lives in the right way—loving God with all our heart, mind, soul and strength, and loving our neighbors as ourselves. Who could ask for a better ending?

Let mutual love continue. (Hebrews 13:1)

Thank You for making love eternal, Gracious God.

The Greatest Evangelist of Love

All too often, we judge people's lives by what they can contribute to the world instead of by their inherent dignity. But *Washington Examiner* writer Tim Carney proved that every life does have value, no matter how powerless that life may seem.

In a column he wrote following the death of his 14-month-old nephew, he said, "John Paul Kilner was born with an advanced case of spinal muscular atrophy. Nearly paralyzed at birth, his body deteriorated further as he grew...Daily saving the life of an immobile kid with a fatal disease raises some fundamental questions. What is the point of such a life?"

Carney's answer: "John Paul lived a superior life. He exuded love...He beamed smiles that made grown men sob.... Also, JP drew love from others. Neighbors, relatives and strangers cooked meals and gave time, equipment and money to help the Kilners.... [His parents] saw John Paul as a blessing, and they generously shared that blessing with the world.... John Paul, who never spoke a word in his life, was the greatest evangelist of love, faith, virtue and hope I have ever met."

He is not here but has risen. (Luke 24:5)

Let all our lives leave a legacy of love, Father.

Undefeated

Violence, poverty, prison and broken families are just a few of the problems facing the players of Memphis, Tennessee's Manassas High School football team. They also haven't won a game in 14 years.

The Christopher Award-winning documentary *Undefeated* chronicles one year of volunteer coach Bill Courtney's tireless efforts to change that sad statistic while offering his players heartfelt compassion and guidance that will lead to success beyond the gridiron.

As Coach Courtney tells his students, "If you...have character, you get to play football. Winning will take care of itself because young men of character and discipline and commitment end up winning in life—and they end up winning in football. But when you flip it and the foundation of what you're doing is football and then you hope all that other stuff follows, then you think football builds character. It does not. Football reveals character."

Endurance produces character, and character produces hope. (Romans 5:4)

Help me develop character and virtue, Holy Spirit.

The Blessing of God and a Mother

When George Washington left his home to become the first President of the United States, his mother's parting words were, "Go, George, go my son, and may the blessing of God and that of a mother be with you always."

This final reassurance by Washington's mother upon his taking the highest office in the land was a fitting climax to the reverence for God which she had instilled in him.

Many a great saint, patriot, writer and others who have been distinguished for service to God and their fellow man, owe a great debt to their usually unsung parents for developing the spirit of greatness within them in a loving way.

Parents are in the best position to nurture in young people the high sense of purpose or vocation which God has implanted in them. These fathers and mothers can do a great service to everybody by training their children to work for the public good in God's name, just as George Washington's mother encouraged him to do.

Wisdom is with the humble. (Proverbs 11:2)

Bless all those who pursue work in public service, Lord. Keep them on the right path.

Turning Stress Into Success

Dr. Denis Waitley offers these three rules for turning stress into success:

- **"Accept the Unchangeable.** Everything that has happened in your life to this minute is unchangeable. It's history. The greatest waste of energy is in looking back at missed opportunities, grudge collecting...and any vengeful thinking. Success is the only acceptable form of revenge. By forgiving your trespassers, you become free to concentrate on going forward with your life and succeeding in spite of your detractors."

- **"Change the Changeable.** What you can change is your reaction to what others say and do. And you can control your own thoughts and actions by dwelling on desired results instead of the penalties of failure. The only real control you have in life is that of your immediate thought and action."

- **"Avoid the Unacceptable.** Get out of the way of potentially dangerous behaviors and environments... involving your health, safety, financial speculation and emotional relationships."

Anxiety weighs down the human heart, but a good word cheers it up. (Proverbs 12:25)

Take the burden of my anxiety onto Your shoulders, Jesus.

Finding Faith in Hollywood

A lifelong Christian and recent convert to the Eastern Orthodox Church, *General Hospital* and *Nashville* star Jonathan Jackson has always been open to talking with people from different religious traditions. He credits God, his parents and Hollywood for that openness.

During an interview on *Christopher Closeup*, Jackson said, "A lot of Christians look at Hollywood as the ultimate evil, but for me, it sharpened my ability to love and appreciate people, no matter where they're at in their lives. I've always been someone who's believed in truth. I don't believe in relativism, a 'your truth, my truth' kind of thing. However, I also believe that the truth must always be spoken in love—and that grace and truth are found in Jesus Christ. So in Hollywood, at a young age, I was thrown into an environment where people were Jewish, atheists, Catholics, different denominations of Protestantism. It helped me to try to find Christ within all of these people, regardless of where they were or what they believed in."

Look for Christ in everyone you meet.

Love your neighbor as yourself. (Matthew 19:19)

May love, not judgment, guide my social interactions, Lord.

Never Too Late to Learn

John Gray, 85, found a new world open up to him after he joined the Spanish club at his assisted living community in West Hartford, Connecticut. He broadened his social circle even as he kept his mind supple.

"In school I thought [Spanish] was a necessary class," he says. "Now it's something I enjoy." Some of Gray's classmates have become his friends and lunch buddies. He's also learning more about Latin American culture.

All this education is keeping Gray and other seniors mentally healthy. *AARP* magazine reports, "Scientists say late-life learning can exercise your mind and help you maintain cognitive functioning."

Some ideas: if you've always done crossword puzzles, try Sudoku. If you've mastered chess, learn bridge. Senior Centers often schedule free or low-cost classes. Look for opportunities to learn new things and meet new people. The idea is to find ways to challenge your brain and nurture your spirit.

He has filled him with divine spirit, with skill... and knowledge in every kind of craft. (Exodus 35:31)

Enable us, Lord, to remain active in the world around us.

Playing a Bad Hand Well

Award-winning *NBC News* correspondent Bob Dotson has always admired people who could work through difficult situations with a positive attitude and an unshakeable determination. That admiration was born out of his own childhood battle with polio, which shrunk the tendon in his left leg, inhibiting his ability to walk.

For almost 10 years, Dotson's mother took him to their local hospital in St. Louis three days a week for therapy. He remembers his doctor giving him the book *The Little Engine That Could,* which was grounded in the message, "I think I can, I know I can." Dotson took that message to heart.

At age 10, doctors performed surgery on him to implant six inches of fake tendon. Now age 66, he notes that "it's still working pretty good" and even allowed him to climb a ladder up the Statue of Liberty for a story many years ago.

On *Christopher Closeup,* Dotson explained the lesson he learned: "Success and thriving…is not a question of just being dealt a good hand; it's playing a bad hand well over and over again."

Endurance produces character. (Romans 5:4)

Lord, help me overcome my afflictions.

The Unknown Soldiers

"In the modern media world, we know the names of Kardashians more than we know the names of U.S. troops who have been killed fighting a war, ostensibly for us."

That's one of the reasons that *CNN* anchor and Chief Washington Correspondent Jake Tapper wrote *The Outpost: An Untold Story of American Valor*, a book that has garnered praise from both liberals and conservatives.

In 2009, Tapper was in the hospital visiting his wife and their day-old son, Jack, when he saw a news report on TV about a combat outpost in Afghanistan that he'd never heard of. It was located at the bottom of three steep mountains near the Pakistan border. Fifty U.S. troops had fought off nearly 400 enemy forces, leaving eight Americans dead.

As Tapper explained on *Christopher Closeup*, "I was holding my son hearing about eight other sons, young men taken from this world. It started me on this journey to find out more."

More of the story tomorrow…

**Give me now wisdom and knowledge.
(2 Chronicles 1:10)**

Open our eyes to the world's important news, Lord.

A Servant Leader in Afghanistan

One of the soldiers featured in Jake Tapper's *The Outpost* is First Lieutenant Ben Keating. On *Christopher Closeup*, Tapper said:

"[Keating] felt he learned more from his Christian Youth Fellowship Leadership training than from Army ROTC. He wanted to be a servant leader like Jesus. When he was a child reading the illustrated Bible, Jesus offering to wash the feet of His disciples was the be-all and end-all of leadership. It [resulted] in a leadership style where he was absolutely beloved by the men under him—and had a prickly relationship with the men over him."

Despite being surrounded by violence and death, Keating's Christian faith was never shaken, though he grew doubtful that America's mission would ever be accomplished. On Nov. 26, 2006, Keating was killed in an accident in Afghanistan. Though Tapper never knew him personally, his death—and the deaths of all the other soldiers he covered—changed the way he approached his job as a journalist.

The conclusion tomorrow...

We are...struck down, but not destroyed. (2 Corinthians 4:8,9)

Bless the families of fallen soldiers, Prince of Peace.

A Soldier's Trials

Covering the number of fallen soldiers featured in his book *The Outpost* took an emotional toll on author Jake Tapper. He explained on *Christopher Closeup,* "It's made me less glib as a person and a journalist. I think that having very brave men cry when they're telling you their stories is a humbling experience. In general, I got to know these [soldiers] through their loved ones and friends...I mourn for them even though I never met them."

That mourning isn't just for the dead, but the survivors as well. Tapper notes that we have hundreds of thousands of veterans who aren't getting the care they need to deal with post-traumatic stress disorder and traumatic brain injuries. Part of the reason is the stigma attached to mental illness which prevents some veterans from seeking the help they need. He hopes his book sheds some light on those problems, resulting in changes for the better.

Tapper adds, "I hope the book provides you with the same window that it provided me in writing it, which is understanding who these people are and being inspired by their selflessness."

The memory of the righteous is a blessing. (Proverbs 10:7)

Inspire us to be people of peace, Heavenly Father.

Tiny Superheroes

In order to do something fun for her young son and nephew, Seattle resident Robyn Rosenberger sewed them both superhero capes. After seeing how much they loved the gift, she decided to make another one for a girl named Brenna, who was fighting a rare congenital skin disease. With a giant, yellow "B" on the cape, Brenna loved it!

After putting a picture of "Super Brenna" on her blog, Rosenberger got requests to send capes to sick children elsewhere. As reported by *ABC News,* she made 700 personalized capes for kids in 45 states and 11 countries over a six-month period. She's even quit her job to meet demand.

Parents of the cape-wearing children point out how great a sense of comfort they provide in a troubling time. That's no surprise to Rosenberger, who says, "These capes are more than fabric. A cape is a visible sign of strength…It lets kids and their family know how extraordinary they really are…Truth is, they are extraordinary because they overcome things we can't imagine—and they do it with a smile."

A cheerful heart is a good medicine.
(Proverbs 17:22)

Help me bring a smile to the sick and lonely, Lord.

Friends: Life's Best Medicine

"There is nothing on earth to be more prized than true friendship." *The Pilot* writer Adam Johnson cites the wisdom of that quote by St. Thomas Aquinas.

"Friends take part in our spiritual existence, mirroring who we are and influencing how we live our lives," Johnson explains. "Recent research suggests that the effects of friendship are also good for our health."

A study at Flinders University in South Australia tracking the lives of over 1,500 senior citizens for 10 years showed that those who had close relationships were 22 percent more likely to live longer than those who didn't.

"When we have friends in our lives, we feel a deeper sense of connectedness with the world," Johnson adds. "Whether you are a social butterfly, or more comfortable with a smaller circle of close confidants, the friendships you nurture today are likely to lead to a longer life down the road."

No matter how old we are, may we always maintain our intimate bonds of friendship.

Two are better than one...For if they fall, one will lift up the other. (Ecclesiastes 4:9-10)

Lord, protect and bless our friends.

Why Can't It Be Us?

Five orphaned siblings from Peru are now living in Blue Springs, Missouri, thanks to the generous and welcoming hearts of Lauren and Scott Sterling.

As reported in *The Daily Mail,* Yhonson, 17, Gerson, 15, Betsi, 12, Joel, 11, and Sibila, nine, had been living in a Peruvian orphanage since their parents died of tuberculosis seven years ago. They insisted on staying together, making the likelihood of adoption slim to none. When a friend of the Sterlings visited the orphanage in 2011, he encouraged the kids to write a letter to them asking if they would adopt them.

Initially, Lauren hoped that someone rich would adopt them, then moved on. But after visiting an orphanage in Guatemala and seeing all the babies without parents, Lauren thought of the kids who sent the letter. She said to Scott, "Somebody's got to do it, why can't it be us? We may eat a lot of spaghetti, I will never buy another $100 pair of jeans again, [but] who cares?"

Out of selflessness and love, a new family was born.

Rescue the oppressed. (Sirach 4:9)

Increase the generosity of our hearts, Lord.

The Trap of Inactivity

In prayer, as in life, it's advisable to take an active rather than a passive approach. Father John Catoir, former Director of The Christophers, preaches this principle in his syndicated column.

"Many people these days fall into the trap of inactivity," Father Catoir observes. "The truth is that, except for salvation itself, God helps those who help themselves."

Father Catoir uses the example of a fictitious man he calls Tom to prove his point. Tom is a man who longs for a job, but makes no concrete effort to look for one. He prays daily for God's help, but does nothing in the meantime. "True prayer is in the will to give ourselves to God," Father Catoir explains. "The will is active in Christian contemplation, not passive."

In other words, don't just sit there hoping for God to change your life for the better; do something to try and make this ideal possible. If you get discouraged, cling to the love of the Lord, a love so great that He sacrificed His only Son to save us from death, giving us the hope and promise of eternal life.

Be doers of the word, and not merely hearers. (James 1:22)

Christ, bless all efforts to improve our lives for the better.

The Dark Knight's Super Heart

Four-year-old Jayden Barber from Youngstown, Ohio, was diagnosed with leukemia in 2010. Despite chemotherapy, the cancer spread to his bones, and Jayden was diagnosed as terminal.

The youngster's greatest wish was to meet the superhero, Batman. Christian Bale, the actor who played Batman in *The Dark Knight* movie trilogy, got wind of Jayden's wish and flew him and his entire family out to Los Angeles for a week's stay. The humble Bale sought no publicity for his act of kindness. It was only revealed when the Barber family posted about it on Facebook.

Jayden's mother, Charlene, wrote: "The entire interaction was like old friends having lunch. Jayden [and Christian] talked movies and superheroes, and he was genuinely happy to hear about everything Jayden wanted to tell him. Christian, his wife and daughter are three of the most beautiful people we have ever met! Christian made these arrangements for us personally and ensured we were treated like royalty."

And the most super news of all? Jayden's terminal cancer has somehow gone into remission.

Seek humility. (Zephaniah 2:3)

Create in me a humble, heroic heart, Divine Savior.

Moving Forward into Eternity

It's been said that time flies when you're having fun. But interestingly enough, time also seems to speed up the minute you officially enter adulthood. Additionally, the harder you fight to beat the clock, the more the days and even years elude you.

"It's like practicing music on a metronome," mother of eight Jaymie Stuart Wolfe writes in *The Pilot*. "No matter how fast I play, it seems as if the beat is always accelerating...When one thing gets done, 10 others rise to take its place."

In the hubbub of this fast-paced world, however, Wolfe insists there is one steady constant we as Christians can rely on to keep us grounded—our Lord's promise of eternal life.

"God is the one who keeps time and eternity," Wolfe concludes. "While we [human beings] live in time here and now, our bodies carry our souls with them...But as we try to orient our lives around the things that last, we ought to remember to count ourselves among them. We are eternal beings."

**God gave us eternal life...in His Son.
(1 John 5:11)**

May we always make time in our busy schedules for our spiritual lives, Jesus, as we look forward to our heavenly salvation.

Music and Joy in the Congo

In 1992, Armand Diangienda, an unemployed pilot in Africa's Congo, decided to create an orchestra because he thought classical music could bring beauty to the bleak, war-torn lives of his countrymen. The only problem? He had no music experience, no musicians, and no instruments. But he didn't let that stop him.

As chronicled in the Christopher Award-winning *60 Minutes* segment *Joy in the Congo,* Diangienda learned to play music himself and recruited several members of his church. Word of his mission spread far and wide, attracting donated instruments and new recruits. Two German opera singers even arrived to teach French-speaking Africans how to sing Italian arias.

Today, Diangienda's dream has become the Kimbanguist Symphony Orchestra. It consists of 200 volunteer musicians and singers, making them the only all-black orchestra in the world—and a testament to the power of determination and hard work.

Begin a song to my God with tambourines, sing to my Lord with cymbals. (Judith 16:1)

Lord, give us the strength and wisdom to achieve our goals.

Measuring Up in the Moment

Author J.R.R. Tolkien wrote the popular books *The Hobbit* and *The Lord of the Rings* series, all of which have been turned into feature films. The stars of *The Hobbit* noted that the stories inherently reflect Tolkien's Christian worldview.

Richard Armitage, who portrays the Dwarf warrior Thorin Oakenshield, said, "One of the things I find when I look into that book [*The Hobbit*] is a sense of Tolkien's Catholicism, his Christianity—not necessarily in a denominational way, but in terms of his chivalric view of the world, his nobility which is expressed through kindness and mercy."

Sir Ian McKellen, who portrays Gandalf the wizard, adds, "The message I think that resonates in the books and films is: Yes, the world is organized by people who are extremely powerful...but they are entirely dependent on the little guy. And [it's impressive] that [Tolkien], who's been through two World Wars, accepts that it's not the great people we build statues to through whom the world is changed—it's the ordinary people who measure up in the moment."

**He leads the humble in what is right.
(Psalm 25:9)**

Help me use my gifts to create a better world, Lord.

A Widow's Worries

With 11 children, the sudden death of her husband, Henry, in 1968 felt like a devastating blow to Alice Keitel. She prayed, "Please help me, Lord. All these kids are depending on me." Though she missed Henry terribly, insurance payments allowed her to stay on their farm in Lost Nation, Iowa, with the kids pitching in to help where they could.

Alice doubted she would ever remarry. However, she admitted to writer Judie Gulley on Patheos.com that she prayed, "Please God, if there is such a man, let him be a good Christian, a man my kids can look up to."

Soon after, a church friend set Alice up with her brother Charlie Lasack, who was a widower. Not only did Charlie and Alice hit it off, but a mutual love developed between him and Alice's kids. On Charlie and Alice's wedding day, one of the children happily exclaimed, "Now we can call him Dad!"

Charlie grounded his family's life in love, God and hard work. When he died in 2010 at age 90, his adopted kids felt grateful that he had chosen to become their father.

Fathers make known to children your faithfulness. (Isaiah 38:19)

Open men's hearts to becoming adoptive fathers, Lord.

I Might Be That Someone

Today, we're sharing a letter from J.F. DeLuca, who's been reading our *Three Minutes a Day* books for 40 years. He writes:

"Forty years ago, the conditions in the neighborhood where I live in the North End of Providence, Rhode Island, were deplorable... Youth were dropping out of school...storefronts were boarded up, senior citizens had no programs or activities available to them...People were saying, 'Someone should do something.' I then remembered the words of The Christophers: It's better to light one candle than to curse the darkness. I realized I might be that 'someone.'

"I gathered four people to form a non-profit...which we named the DaVinci Center for Community Progress...We now serve more than 5,000 people with social services including adult education, daily meals for senior citizens, youth programs, etc.

"I received my initial inspiration from *Three Minutes a Day* and I continue...to get some great ideas for new programs from your publication. Keep up the great work. Who knows where the daily seeds you sow will take root?"

Serve one another. (1 Peter 4:10)

Inspire me to take opportunities to serve, Father.

Life Lessons from Racquetball

Some of the greatest lessons Steve Goodier learned from playing racquetball weren't about the game, but about life. He shared a few of them on his website LifeSupportSystem.com.

- "On the court, those who lose their focus, lose games. In life, people who are too distracted by yesterday's regrets or tomorrow's problems will never experience the joy of today."

- "When playing doubles, cooperation is essential. No team, no family, no nation will succeed that is plagued with internal squabbling."

- "There are always people who will do better than you. But your job is not to be the best. If you simply strive to be YOUR best, you will have succeeded."

- "It isn't over until the last point is scored. Many victories are snatched after one comes back from almost insurmountable odds. So it is with life."

- "In racquetball, the only way to score is to serve. Likewise, service is key to life. Individuals and institutions that make a difference find ways to serve others."

O simple ones, learn prudence. (Proverbs 8:5)

Help me grow in wisdom and holiness, Holy Spirit.

Praying Before Oatmeal

Mary DeTurris Poust was a multitasker, used to mindlessly eating breakfast while reading e-mails on her laptop or focusing on the *New York Times* crossword puzzle. Then, while on a retreat that didn't allow reading, writing, or talking, she was confronted by the mealtime dilemma, "It's just me and my corn chowder. I've got to figure out what to do here."

That incident forced DeTurris Poust to eat mindfully, even prayerfully, paying attention to each bite of food and how it tasted. It also helped lead to her book, *Cravings: A Catholic Wrestles with Food, Self-Image and God.*

Though DeTurris Poust initially fell back into her old habits when she returned home, she made a conscious effort to follow through on what she learned. As she explained on *Christopher Closeup,* "I took everything off the table, lit a candle, and started to pray before I ate oatmeal. Now I talk about it as my 'mindful oatmeal.' And I still try to do that practice every day…to do everything with that sense of reverence…It makes you full, not just in a physical way, but in a spiritual way."

Is not life more than food? (Matthew 6:25)

Help me to eat mindfully and prayerfully, Lord.

Stop Repeating Angry Stories

Anger is a normal human emotion, but sometimes we can let it consume us and block our own happiness. Why? Because we mentally relive the reason for our anger over and over again.

Dr. Gail Brenner calls this repeating our "angry stories." She writes, "Angry stories barrel through our minds like an out-of-control train careening down the tracks. To find freedom from anger, you must recognize the story and see that repeating it doesn't serve you. Yes, what happened happened. But how much longer are you going to let it be your ball and chain?"

She offers strategies for moving beyond your angry stories:

- "Open up with compassion to all involved, including yourself."
- "Recognize that you are bringing the past into the present by repeating the story endlessly."
- "Bring your full attention into the sensations you are experiencing in the moment."
- "Commit to bringing all your actions in alignment with what you really, really want."

Whoever is slow to anger has great understanding, but...a hasty temper exalts folly. (Proverbs 14:29)

Instill me with Your peace when I'm angry, Jesus.

Small Moments of Joy

"Far too often, it takes a catastrophe to make us appreciate what we had," writes Gretchen Rubin in *Good Housekeeping* magazine. That's why she has chosen to work "at finding happiness in the small, ordinary details in life and appreciating the adventure of everyday existence."

For instance, instead of overlooking "minor but satisfying joys like a sunny morning or the fact that my husband has cleaned up the kitchen," Rubin makes it a point to voice her gratitude. Because it isn't easy to stay focused on everyday joys, she relies on simple rituals to help.

For example, when she crosses the threshold into her apartment, she stops and consciously expresses happiness at being able to return to a wonderful family and a cozy home. She also notes, "Giving thanks before meals is one of the most universal ways of incorporating gratitude into everyday life."

Make it a point to incorporate gratitude strategies into your life as well.

And now, our God, we give thanks to You and praise Your glorious name. (1 Chronicles 29:13)

Thank You, Lord, for daily moments of joy.

A Thanksgiving Proclamation

Imitation of the "deep religious convictions of those who formed our nation" was the underlying theme of President Dwight D. Eisenhower's message for Thanksgiving Day, 1957.

Calling on all Americans to observe the occasion in a religious spirit, he said in his Thanksgiving Proclamation:

"It behooves us to dwell upon the deep religious convictions of those who formed our nation out of a wilderness, and to recall that our leaders throughout the succeeding generations have relied upon Almighty God for vision and strength of purpose...

"As a nation we have prospered; we are enjoying the fruit of our land and the product of our toil; we are making progress in our efforts to translate our national ideals into living realities...For such blessings let us be devoutly thankful, and at the same time let us be sensitive and responsive to the obligations which such great mercies entail."

Do not worry about anything, but in everything by prayer and supplication with thanksgiving let your requests be made known to God. (Philippians 4:6)

Thank You, Father, for our blessings.

The Other First Thanksgiving

The pilgrims weren't the first to celebrate Thanksgiving with Native Americans, writes Los Angeles Archbishop Jose H. Gomez in his book *Immigration and the Next America*. In fact, missionary priests from Spain were the first to do so in 1565.

Four priests, including Father López de Mendoza Grajales, traveled to what is now St. Augustine, Florida, with the explorer Pedro Menéndez de Avilés. They landed on Sept. 8, the date on which Catholics celebrate the birth of Mary, the mother of Jesus.

Archbishop Gomez writes, "Father López said he and his brother priests...planted a large cross in the sand. Then all the crew marched up to the cross, knelt down before it and kissed it...A crowd of native people gathered on the beach and they began doing what they saw the missionaries doing—kneeling and kissing the cross themselves. After that, the priests celebrated a solemn Mass in honor of the Nativity of Mary. Then they all sat down together with the natives and ate a thanksgiving meal."

People in every age should express gratitude to the Creator.

I will magnify Him with thanksgiving. (Psalm 69:30)

Fill my heart with gratitude, Father.

On the Path

On a sunny Saturday morning, everyone in one New York City neighborhood seemed to be out for a walk—including Carole. As she made her way down the main street, she met a friend whose brother had just died. Expressing her sympathy, Carole offered a hug and a listening ear before moving on.

Next, Carole saw two children on their way to the store for their grandmother who had just had surgery. Catching up on the grandmother's progress, Carole sent the youth off with a message of prayerful greetings for a complete and quick recovery.

Finishing her walk, she came upon an elderly neighbor, who needed a hand carrying two large bags of groceries. Carole made a detour before going home, walking and talking with the man, enjoying the sunshine.

Who will the Lord place in your path this day? How will you offer them His loving heart?

You show me the path of life. In Your presence there is fullness of joy; in Your right hand are pleasures forevermore. (Psalm 16:11)

Help me to see Your face, Lord, in all I meet today.

Get a Dog?

There are a lot of reports that pets can be good for our health. *AARP* magazine cites statistics showing that "Fido" can help your fitness efforts. How?

"Dog owners who routinely take their pooches for strolls get an extra hour of activity per week...Also noteworthy: The oldest dog walkers—those age 65-plus—walk their dogs longer than any other age group."

Dogs have a way of making their needs known and, as such, might offer us the needed motivation to get moving.

If you don't have a dog or are unable to manage one full-time, perhaps you can volunteer at a shelter or offer to walk a friend's pooch. But caring for any kind of pet can have salutary effects. Be open to the healing aspects of life with all God's creatures.

So out of the ground the Lord God formed every animal of the field and every bird of the air. (Genesis 2:19)

Father, bless those who care for all of Your creation.

Advent: Time to Consider What You Value

"Advent is...a time for taking stock, for looking to the coming year with hope," writes the *Catholic News Service's* Daniel S. Mulhall. "Advent is when we should take time to consider what we truly value."

There are several methods Mulhall recommends we use to fully utilize the beauty and potential of Advent:

- Say a prayer for every person whom you consider a "blessing in your life."
- Search for beauty in every aspect of your life—"let it fill up your soul and lift your spirits."
- Make an effort to make new friends.
- Be attentive to someone who truly needs your help. God speaks to us every day, often through others—may we be wise enough to listen.
- Work on your spiritual life as you would a regular diet. Pray more, worry less.

Above all, remember that Jesus is the reason for the season.

Do not store up...treasures on earth...but store up for yourselves treasures in heaven. (Matthew 6:19-20)

Lord, grant us a peaceful and blessed Advent.

Man of Science, Man of Faith

Though he cares for disabled children and adults who are malformed or crippled, orthopedic surgeon Dr. Joseph Dutkowsky sees the image and likeness of God in each of them.

During an interview on the *PBS* show *Religion and Ethics Newsweekly*, this man of science, who works at New York-Presbyterian Hospital and an upstate clinic, revealed that his work is grounded in his Catholic faith. He said, "People don't need for me to preach at them. They need for me to care...to walk in with the love of God and to try and share it in any way that I can."

Sometimes, that approach simply requires listening. Patient Chris Rosa said, "A lot of doctors don't listen. They want to do what they gotta do and go away. Just because we may look funny doesn't mean you should talk over us."

That won't happen with Dr. Dutkowsky, who said, "Even if I can't cure the condition, if they're being overburdened with that cross [and] I can just hold up a corner, it might make it light enough for them to be able to carry it and move on."

Bear one another's burdens. (Galatians 6:2)

Give me the strength to help carry someone's cross, Jesus.

A Positive Christmas

This season, try something positive. Instead of getting angry at the increasing avoidance of "Christmas" in favor of "Happy Holidays," skip the confrontation and pretend this message comes from Jesus:

If you want to celebrate My birthday, don't bother writing letters of protest. Send letters of love and hope instead.

Visit someone in a nursing home. (They'll appreciate it!) Pick someone who has hurt you in the past, and forgive him or her.

Don't nitpick about what the local retailer calls Christmas, and be patient with the people who work there. Give them a warm smile and a kind word. Even if they can't wish you a merry Christmas, you can wish them one.

Support a missionary—someone who takes My love and Good News to those who have never heard My name.

Finally, if you really want to make a statement, behave like a Christian. Let your actions show that you are one of Mine!

For all who are led by the Spirit of God are children of God. (Romans 8:14)

Abba, may the meaning of Christmas reside in our hearts all year.

No Greater Gift

Last Christmas, 23-year-old Michael Crowe of Omaha, Nebraska, was especially thankful for his unexpected gift—a second chance at life.

In August 2012, Michael's stomach flu escalated into a serious heart condition diagnosed as myocarditis, an inflammation of the heart muscle. Crowe was told he would need a heart transplant right away, and his family started praying for one to be found. But much to their delight and the doctor's relief, Michael's heart miraculously "healed itself," and the transplant was unnecessary.

Michael Crowe credits his recovery to the Lord and the hundreds of people praying for him, not just among his family and friends, but all over the country, thanks to a website his family created to provide updates on his condition.

"There have been times when I have questioned how much God played a role in my day-to-day life," he told *Catholic Voice* reporter Lisa Maxson. "But after my experience, I realize God is always present, and His miracles come in many different forms."

We do not know how to pray...but that very Spirit intercedes with sighs. (Romans 8:26-27)

Lord, help us to recognize the power of everyday miracles.

How to Lose and Find $5,000

Don't you hate it when you accidentally throw away $5,000? Magda Castillo of Queens, New York, sure wasn't happy with herself when she did that exact thing.

Castillo had gotten rid of her old refrigerator, forgetting that she had hidden $5,000 in one of its doors. Panicked, she headed to the recycling center that had picked up the fridge and told the worker in charge what happened. As reported by the *Daily News,* he couldn't find it so Castillo made the sign of the cross and left, assuming the money was gone forever.

When employee Mike Downer arrived for work and heard the story from his co-worker, he remembered the refrigerator, found it on-site, and took out the money so he could return it. Castillo didn't leave her number so they alerted the media, hoping she would hear the story on the news. Sure enough, she did.

A grateful Castillo insisted Downer accept a $300 reward for his initiative and honesty. Then she opened a bank account to ensure this kind of incident never happens again.

Honesty comes home to those who practice it. (Sirach 27:9)

May I always choose honesty, Heavenly Father.

Operation Mend

Army Sgt. Jason March had always liked being in photographs, but the Iraqi sniper's bullet that shattered his face stole that pleasure from his life. Though surgeons reconstructed his face and head, March was no longer able to smile because of a severed nerve. That's where Operation Mend came in.

Based at UCLA, Operation Mend consists of a group of cosmetic surgeons who perform advanced facial and hand surgeries for severely scarred veterans. As reported by the *Inland Valley Daily Bulletin,* 88 vets have come through the program so far, some requiring up to 50 corrective surgeries. Many veterans don't take advantage of the program because they're sick of having surgeries or because they feel worthless. Sgt. March, however, was willing to make the effort.

By taking a nerve from his calf muscle and attaching it to his face, doctors gave him the ability to smile again. March, who underwent a total of 80 surgeries after his injury, said, "Operation Mend gave me back my morale...This organization started a whole new world for soldiers."

He restores my soul. (Psalm 23:3)

Mend the wounds of our bodies and souls, Divine Healer.

Christmas Love for a Crabby Grump

Some people have co-workers that are mean, but Jen McKinney describes a former colleague as "really mean." Though she dreaded crossing paths with this crabby grump, she had no choice.

When the joy-filled season of Christmas approached, McKinney didn't want her good mood ruined, so she decided to try a new approach with this woman: kindness.

As McKinney told *Catholic Digest's* Rachel Balducci, "I gave her a simple present—a sweater—with a note about the season from St. Nicholas on his feast day. I didn't sign it, but she was so excited, and she wore that sweater until it came apart, never knowing who it came from."

McKinney's lesson fit the spirit of the season: "It was wonderful for me to show love to someone not easy to love. I saw her as a child of God instead of a brute."

It may take a lot of effort and prayer, but try treating the unlovable people in your life as lovable children of God.

Steadfast love and faithfulness will meet; righteousness and peace will kiss. (Psalm 85:10)

Give me the grace to deal with negativity, Jesus.

A Spiritually Fruitful Advent

We generally think of Lent as the time to take on extra tasks out of love for God, but Advent can be just as spiritually fruitful. It may even be more vital because the hustle and bustle of the holiday season can leave us frazzled and distracted. A conscious effort on our part to remember the coming Christ-child can keep us grounded in the true meaning of the season.

God's love for us will never go away, regardless of whether we engage in a relationship with Him or not. He's good that way, much more patient and understanding than we are. But if we never take the time to express gratitude to the Creator for all our blessings, how good a relationship can we expect to have?

If your relationship with God is feeling lackluster lately, take the opportunity to return His love on a more regular basis. Offer words of praise, not just petition. And take time out to just "be" with each other. You may come to experience God's love in a new, more satisfying way.

I waited patiently for the Lord; He inclined to me and heard my cry. (Psalm 40:1)

Holy Spirit, open my heart to the grace that the Christ-Child will bring.

Theology Behind Bars

Catholics, Protestants, Buddhists and a Rastafarian sit in Father George Williams' theology class. But this isn't an ordinary classroom; it's California's San Quentin State Prison.

The Jesuit priest who serves as the prison's Catholic chaplain began the program in 2012 to help inmates interested in learning more about Catholicism. Response has been positive.

Johnny, a student in Father Williams' class who's been behind bars for 16 years, was baptized Catholic in 2010. He explained to *America* magazine's Kerry Weber, "The Catholic Church [is] where I felt most comfortable. Maybe that's because of the family setting here, with the Father and with Virgin Mary as our mother and all the angels and saints."

What has he gotten out of Father Williams' classes? "The more I meditate on things I'm doing in the church program, the better I am at learning more about who I used to be, how I'm different now and what caused me to do what I did to get here."

Study the history and wisdom of your faith.

Give me...wisdom and knowledge.
(2 Chronicles 1:10)

Increase my understanding of Your teachings, Jesus.

Steps for a Stronger Family

As Jesus was born into a good family, He desires His children to be part of strong families too. Writer Lauren Gulde offers these suggestions to build the bonds between mothers, fathers and children.

- Create a prayer intention list for the month: As a family, write a list of intentions, then remember them each night during prayer time.

- Learn about faith together: have a family Scripture study or watch videos like Father Robert Barron's Christopher Award-winning *Catholicism* series.

- Family Fun Nights: play games; cook together; watch a movie; read together; play outside or go on a walk.

- Travel: go to local museums; plan a day trip.

- Family Service Projects: Volunteer together at Church ministries, community projects, or pregnancy centers.

- Family Meetings: Discuss projects, special events, prayer requests.

And in your descendants all the families of the earth shall be blessed. (Acts 3:25)

Jesus, through the example of Your parents Mary and St. Joseph, help families be strong in love.

Christmas Really Does Change Everything

Christmas isn't only the season for giving gifts and decorating trees—it's also a time to curl up on the couch with a mug of hot cocoa and watch one of the many heartwarming holiday movies on TV.

While these films are spiritually uplifting in their own ways, showing Christmas as a time when people renew their faith in themselves and each other, their source of belief often rests not in the Nativity but rather in the figure of Santa Claus.

"These Christmas fantasy movies rarely mention the reason for the season," Dale O'Leary observes in *The Pilot*. "In one way, they represent a paganization of Christmas...without Christ—and yet there is a truth hidden in these fantasies: Christmas really does change everything. We are called to believe not in a jolly, white-bearded man with flying reindeer, but in something far more wonderful—a virgin mother of God's son—God come down from heaven as a helpless child."

Never forget the true meaning of Christmas—the birth of Christ, the source of salvation for us all.

For a child has been born for us. (Isaiah 9:6)

Jesus, may we remember Your humble entry into our world.

The Unlikely Musical Genius

When Patrick Henry Hughes was born crippled and without eyes, his parents were devastated. They decided to persevere, though, and their patience was rewarded a year later when the baby was able to sit at a piano keyboard. He could hit any note on demand, and by his second birthday was taking requests for simple tunes like "You Are My Sunshine."

As the years went on he could play standards and classical pieces, and his Mother and Dad realized they had a musical genius on their hands.

Now Patrick is a freshman at the University of Louisville, and, with his father's help, is a member of the marching band. His Dad attends classes with him, too, a schedule made possible by working the graveyard shift at UPS from 11 p.m. to 6 a.m.

"So I was born crippled and without eyes," Patrick says. "Big deal! I have musical gifts and a great opportunity to meet new people."

"He's my hero," says his Dad. "He's taught me I don't have any complaints."

He...strengthens the powerless. (Isaiah 40:29)

Abba, may we never take our life's blessings for granted.

Catching the Bus

Jackie had been insanely busy at work. Early morning arrivals at the office each day were matched to late evening departures. And then there was answering e-mails almost through the night.

In the brief time she was with her husband and daughter, she never felt present to them—or to herself.

One day on the way to work, she met a neighbor who mentioned taking the early bus that night back home. Jackie vowed to do the same. She texted her daughter, and the two met and traveled home on that bus. Then they went shopping.

Her husband joined the pair later for dinner at their favorite neighborhood restaurant. As they laughed and talked, Jackie realized how much she had been missing—and pledged to catch that early bus more often than not.

Work's responsibilities are important, but so are the chores of the heart—the task of engagement with family and friends.

**Love one another deeply from the heart.
(1 Peter 1:22)**

Be never far from me, Lord.

Best Friends

Thanks to champion dog trainer Shannon Walker from Vancouver, Washington, military veterans suffering from post-traumatic stress disorder (PTSD) are finding mental and emotional healing with a little help from the animal world.

Walker prepares canines to be companion animals for vets with PTSD. For instance, former Army gunner Kevin Williams, 26, would "wake from nightmares, grab my gun and search the room in fear. Now I open my eyes, see Sammy [his Labrador] sleeping soundly and I know I'm safe." Randy Guillory, a Vietnam vet, holds the paw of his pit bull Leia at night. If he trembles, she licks his face in comfort.

"Having a dog can totally change a person's outlook," says Walker, who runs Northwest Battle Buddies, the nonprofit which provides veterans with their service animals. "When I hand over an animal to a veteran, I know that both the dog and the owner will respect, protect and love each other. It's an awesome moment—and the beginning of an incredible relationship."

Even though I walk through the darkest valley, I fear no evil; for You are with me. (Psalm 23:4)

May we appreciate the value of companionship, Jesus.

Rosaries for Newtown

In the aftermath of the Sandy Hook school shootings in 2012, which killed 26 students and teachers, Newtown, Connecticut residents needed extra comfort and prayers. To that end, Sandy Hook alumna Jackie Hennessey came up with the idea of making rosaries, using her parish of Holy Family in Endwell, New York, as a fundraising springboard for her project.

"Everyone wanted to help," Hennessey told *The Catholic Sun.* "The thought of creating rosaries that would actually touch the kids who lost brothers, sisters, cousins and friends, well, that's pretty powerful."

Hennessey's charitable act is also a family affair. Her mother, Pam Arsenault, is the director of parish education at St. Rose of Lima Church in Newtown. She distributed over 1,800 rosaries to the Sandy Hook children on Good Friday.

"The gift of the rosaries will help the process of healing," Arsenault said. "We say in Newtown that we choose love, not hate. This is a tremendous gift of love."

Pray for one another, so that you may be healed. (James 5:16)

Lord, comfort those who mourn the losses of loved ones.

Santa versus Sandy

After seeing news coverage of people whose homes were destroyed by Superstorm Sandy in October 2012, a wealthy businessman from Kansas City, Missouri, traveled to Staten Island, New York, to play Santa Claus for those in need.

The anonymous Secret Santa arrived with $100 bills to distribute to whoever needed them. He began at a Salvation Army thrift store, and also visited a Veterans of Foreign Wars hall where meals and cleaning supplies were being handed out.

A law enforcement official who traveled around the borough with Secret Santa told the *New York Post*, "His generosity was matched only by his ability to connect with people from all walks of life before he pulled out the $100 bills."

Secret Santa felt good about his mission too. He said, "It's not about the gift of giving money. It's about the gift of joy you give yourself when you give to others...I want to recruit other executives and CEOs to act as Secret Santas in different cities."

For to the one who pleases Him God gives wisdom and knowledge and joy.
(Ecclesiastes 2:26)

Father, may I reflect Your holy, loving and giving nature to those around me.

The Bar That Helps Santa

Every Christmas season, Kip's Inn in Milwaukee, Wisconsin, doesn't just serve drinks; it serves the less fortunate in the community.

As reported in *The Catholic Herald,* owner Kim Engebregtsen grew up as one of five children in a poor family that was helped by the generosity of other people and the Catholic Church. As a means of repaying that kindness, she's sponsored an annual toy collection for Catholic Charities at the bar for the last six years.

Each year, Catholic Charities gives Engebregtsen a list with wishes from needy families that she and her patrons go above and beyond to fulfill. They don't just buy what's asked for; they include a little extra. Sharon Brumer, communications manager of an appreciative Catholic Charities, said of Engebregtsen, "She embraces sharing and giving to others, and that always rubs off on the people that come to your establishment."

It sounds like Engebregtsen exemplifies the joy of giving, the joy we're all supposed to feel at the gift of God's Son.

The righteous are generous. (Psalm 37:21)

Holy Spirit, inspire our generosity.

Finding the Familiar Far Away

A little girl from Israel fearfully entered her new first-grade classroom in New York City. Everything looked different and sounded different.

Her father spoke to the teacher, explaining that they had just arrived in New York, and that his daughter was learning English, but slowly. Overhearing the conversation, another first-grader—her own father from Israel, and her mother from New York—approached her new classmate.

In perfect Hebrew, she said to the frightened child, "Welcome to our school! I will be your friend!"

The two children hugged, smiling, while the father cried, joyfully relieved.

Love is a universal language—with the power to transform fear into hope, sadness into joy.

Come in, my daughter, and welcome. Blessed be your God who has brought you to us. (Tobit 11:17)

I reach out to You, Lord, in my darkest hour, seeking the blessing of Your peace.

Defending "Merry Christmas"

For all those who fear the loss of Christ in Christmas, take heart. At least one person of another faith harbors no objection to a "Merry Christmas!" at this time of year. Here's how Ben Stein, the well-known commentator, expressed it (in part) recently on *CBS:*

"I am a Jew...and it does not bother me even a little bit when people call those beautiful, lit up, bejeweled trees Christmas trees. I don't feel threatened. I don't feel discriminated against. That's what they are, Christmas trees.

"It doesn't bother me...when people say 'Merry Christmas' to me. I don't think they are slighting me or getting ready to put me in a ghetto. In fact, I kind of like it. It shows that we are all brothers and sisters celebrating this happy time of year...

"I don't like getting pushed around for being a Jew, and I don't think Christians like getting pushed around for being Christians. I think people who believe in God are sick and tired of getting pushed around, period."

Heartening words at any time of year.

There is neither Jew nor Greek...for all of you are one in Jesus Christ. (Galatians 3:28)

Father, let nothing separate us from Your divine love.

Fortunate Fall

"I've been meditating on the poverty and the wealth of being human for some time now. The poverty of need—our desperate need for redemption, salvation, and mercy—and the wealth of knowing Christ as Redeemer through those needs."

That's the motivation for singer/songwriter Audrey Assad's latest album, entitled *Fortunate Fall*. Her goal is to create a work of art that fits into the Church's tradition of beauty.

Assad explained, "I have long believed that true Beauty can change a world where truth and goodness are no longer important to most people. Beauty is still idolized in our society, and so it still has influence, however warped its role may have become. But the remarkable thing about true Beauty is that, when it is real and when it is pure, it carries in itself Truth and Goodness. The three are inseparable. And the best thing I can do as an artist who wants to serve the Church is to love all three, and to pursue them with prayer and humility, hoping to offer them to the Church and the world using the gifts I've been given."

I was overjoyed to find some of your children walking in the truth. (2 John 1:4)

Make me an outlet of your creative genius, Lord.

Nice Running Into You

In his column in *The Catholic Review* of Baltimore, Father Joe Breighner recently told one of those hard-to-get-out-of-your-mind stories that's well, hard to get out of your mind! He was stopped at a traffic light years ago when another driver—a young man, stoned on drugs—plowed into him. The young man was arrested, Father Breighner was unhurt, and that was that.

Until recently that is, when the remorseful man reappeared at a retreat and asked to speak to the priest. You don't know the full story behind that incident, Father Breighner was told by this figure from his past. The young man that day intended to drive to the cemetery, overdose on all the drugs he had with him, and die on his mother's grave. The accident saved him, and, according to the penitent, he's remained off drugs and alcohol for 30 years.

"It's easy to forget that our God is a God of surprises," the priest wrote. "Our job in life is not to work 'for' God; our job is to allow God to work through us. And when someone says, 'It was nice running into you,' it will have a whole new meaning."

The Lord has made everything for its purpose. (Proverbs 16:11)

Lord, remind us that everything happens for a reason.

Charlie's Promise

When he was a seventh-grader in Cleveland, Sean Patrick remembers a new arrival to the neighborhood: Charlie Carroll from the mining area of West Virginia. Charlie had a perpetual smile on his face, and was quickly welcomed into Sean's circle of friends.

Prior to Christmas, Charlie revealed that he needed to find someone for whom he could perform a good deed. The reason? After his father escaped a mine collapse a few years earlier, Charlie made a promise to God to help someone every Christmas season as a sign of gratitude. That year, he chose to paint the apartment walls of Mr. Stolarski, a wheelchair-bound senior.

Sean and his friends were so taken by the idea that they adopted Charlie's promise as well, performing good deeds that Christmas—and every one since then.

Writing in *Catholic Digest,* Sean notes that Charlie went on to become Father Charles Carroll, "a Holy Cross priest and missionary in Bangladesh." He hopes the good deeds that Charlie inspired are making the Holy Family smile.

Clothe yourselves with compassion. (Colossians 3:12)

To honor Your birth, Jesus, I choose to share my blessings.

Like the Face of God

In May 2012, singer-songwriter Brooke White gave birth to her and her husband Dave's first child: a daughter named London. Becoming a mom has added a richness and joy to White's life that she'd never experienced before.

During an interview on *Christopher Closeup* about her album *White Christmas,* she said, "I had just gotten home from New York and performing at the Rockefeller Center tree lighting. I laid London down to take a nap and she locked eyes with me...I was stressed out and a little overwhelmed—and she looked at me and, truly, it was like the face of God. It's like she was telling me, 'This is what's important, and it's okay.'"

White continued, "That was such a blessing. I needed it in that moment. Since she was born, everything shifted in my mind. I know most every parent goes through some sort of transformation, but for me it was instant with London. She came out not crying; her eyes were open, and she was this alert little person ready to live. I can't wait to see this little person blossom and grow. I love her. She's perfect. She is love."

Their children become a blessing. (Psalm 37:26)

Bring joy to all mothers, Lord.

The Christmas Miracle

It was Christmas Eve in London; the year was 1940. A young German student, severely afflicted with pneumonia, begged English nurse Eve Gordon to keep him awake for the night, for if he fell asleep, he knew he would not survive.

Taking pity on the student, Eve spent the night regaling him with the beloved Christmas story and singing him holiday carols. The young man remained awake, and was released from the hospital days later, fully recovered.

Several years passed and Hitler's terrifying Nazi regime swept across Europe. Gordon's language skills earned her a position as a spy in Nazi-occupied Norway. When she and many other Norwegian citizens were caught one day, Eve feared the worst and prayed for a quick death, lest her mission be discovered.

Roughly pushed into a room for questioning, Eve was shocked to recognize her Nazi interrogator as the student she helped years ago. Knowing Gordon as well, the soldier pointed to the door: "Go. I give you back your Christmas."

Love your enemies, do good. (Luke 6:35)

Lord, may we give as generously as we receive.

The King of Kings Is Always With You

In his book *A Simple Guide to Happiness*, former Director of The Christophers Father John Catoir tells the following story:

"In 1953, I was walking guard duty at midnight on Christmas Eve. There I was, a lonely Army draftee serving at Fort Sam Houston in San Antonio, Texas...I could hear the choir singing at the post chapel, where Midnight Mass was being held, and I felt terribly lonely.

"It never dawned on me that I was giving in to self-pity, and thereby was missing a wonderful opportunity to come closer to God. It would have been so much better had I united spiritually with the choir and thought of God as a friend who was closer to me than my own heartbeat.

"I didn't realize that joy never comes to those who are caught up in their own brooding...The thoughts you think soon become the emotions you feel. If you think you're alone in the world, your feelings of loneliness will intensify. But you are never alone. Your best friend, the King of kings, is always with you."

In Your presence there is fullness of joy. (Psalm 16:11)

Lord, help me to choose joy when I'm tempted by self-pity.

Reviving Christmas

Though many of us consider reading or watching Charles Dickens' *A Christmas Carol* as an annual tradition, the story was written at a time when the opposite was true.

As recounted by Jamie Lutton in *The Capitol Hill Times,* "When Charles Dickens wrote *A Christmas Carol* in 1842, the holiday was nearly dead in modern England. Christmas was celebrated by the rural and poor, but frowned upon by employers."

It was only after reading author Washington Irving's lament that people were losing the "goodwill and cheerfulness" of the holiday that Dickens felt inspired to write a story about it.

As he walked the streets of London seeing poor, starving children, Dickens grew angry that many of the city's wealthy citizens saw them as "surplus population," as unnecessary human beings instead of as children of God. He incorporated that theme into his story, reminding his readers that the birth of Jesus is a time of celebration and appreciation of all human life.

Do not despise one of these little ones...Their angels continually see the face of My Father. (Matthew 18:10)

Jesus, help children to experience love.

A Healing Presence

"All through our lives, we need the healing presence of others; perhaps a grandmother, perhaps a therapist; someone when the going gets rough, with whom to share tears and smiles."

Judith Schmidt, Ph.D., learned that significant life lesson as a little girl, while spending many Sunday afternoons at her grandmother's home. She describes the atmosphere as "a warming world away from the warring one at home."

That early example taught Dr. Schmidt what children need in order to become adults capable of love. She herself grew up to become a clinical psychologist who wants to help people.

All these years later, Dr. Schmidt still returns to that place of comfort in her memory. She says, "I know that there will be a moment when my grandmother will call my name. In the kitchen, we will sit quietly together....She will put her hand to my face, smile and touch me with love."

Rash words are like sword thrusts, but the tongue of the wise brings healing. (Proverbs 12:18)

Jesus, may we fully appreciate the healing power of love.

Rain to the Rescue!

Man's best friend can also prove to be a wonderful spiritual healer. Just ask Father Bert Woolson, who has a five-year-old female King Shepherd dog named Rain. A member of the Indiana Division of Mental Health and Addictions' K-9 Assisted Crisis Response Team, Rain was originally trained to be a wheelchair assistance dog. Father Bert, a State Police Chaplain, adopted her, making her a part of his "special ministry."

The chaplain's main task is comforting people at accident scenes, and helping them find the proper mental and spiritual care in the aftermath. According to Father Bert, Rain is a superbly instinctive canine caregiver.

"She was in Henryville (following a tornado in March) for two days...We also responded to a fire," the priest recalls. "When a fireman injured his arm, somehow that dog gave him the courage to go on. I have no idea how she did it."

Animal behaviorists tell us that just touching a dog can greatly lower a person's stress level. How fortunate we are that God has blessed us with such uncannily perceptive companions!

But ask the animals, and they will teach you. (Job 12:7)

Abba, bless and protect faithful pets, our unsung healers.

Seeing Sunsets from a New Perspective

An anonymous author once shared the following thoughts on dealing with change:

"It is easy to affirm divine order when all is going smoothly, but it can be more difficult when I experience a loss. Divine order is a continual process. I know that when the sun sets on one side of the world, it is rising on the other.

"When I consider my life in this way, I see my own sunsets from a new perspective. I accept and honor the transitions in my life. I allow what was once part of my experience to pass, and I wait patiently for what is next.

"As I move through change, I am not alone. The love of God is my assurance and support. With God, I gain a deeper understanding of my life. I know that after every sunset, I will experience a grand sunrise."

He will wipe every tear from their eyes...And the one who was seated on the throne said, "See, I am making all things new." (Revelation 21:4,5)

Abba, guide us through life's difficult transitions.

A Good Samaritan Needs Help Himself

When Hurricane Sandy whipped through the East Coast in October 2012, Pete Vadola's home in Staten Island, New York, was one of the few left standing in his neighborhood of Midland Beach. Vadola came through for his stricken neighbors, though, evacuating no less than 200 of them with a motorboat.

Now Vadola—who lives with his wife Melissa and their two young sons—knows how the others feel. His own home was destroyed by fire in July of 2013, and Vadola's family had to take up lodging in his parents' house nearby.

"When a friend who was marooned in his attic with his wife and kid called for help the day after Sandy, I felt blessed that my home was spared," he told Denis Hamill of the *Daily News*. "Now I know how all of my neighbors felt."

He's keeping everything in perspective, though. "Thank God no one was hurt. I have insurance; I have a job. I'm okay. But I am deeply touched by my neighbors, who care so much about us. That's why, like everybody else around here, I will rebuild."

I will be with them in trouble. (Psalm 91:15)

Redeemer, may we reach out to those who helped us in our need.

How to Keep Your New Year's Resolutions

How many times do we make our New Year's resolutions with the best of intentions, but then end up breaking them?

Father Pat Toner, pastor of St. Joseph's Church in Plain City, Ohio, offers some useful tips for sticking to your resolutions in *The Catholic Times:*

- Limit your number of resolutions to one or two. Trying to keep one resolution is hard enough without having to juggle too many at once.

- Replace your bad habit with a new, more beneficial task. For example, if you find yourself taking God's name in vain, turn your cursing into a prayer to Him.

- Make it a daily intention. Try to include this new habit as a part of your everyday ritual.

- Develop strategies to ingrain the habit. For instance, if you have trouble praying in the evening, like Father Pat, putting your hymnal on your bedside table might help.

I can do all things through Him who strengthens me. (Philippians 4:13)

Jesus, may our faith be at the center of every New Year's resolution.

Prepare for New Possibilities

Patheos.com blogger Deacon Greg Kandra and his wife spent one New Year's Eve in a Times Square hotel, overlooking the revelry and confetti below. The next morning, they were amazed at how well the streets had been cleaned up.

Deacon Greg then saw those clean streets as a symbol for New Year's Day—and a symbol of Mary, the mother of Jesus.

He wrote, "New Year's Day is...the moment when everything is possible. Every page of the calendar is blank. Every diet is successful... Here and now we begin anew. How appropriate, then, that the Church...has dedicated this particular moment in time to Our Lady, as we mark the feast of Mary the Mother of God. In Mary, we see the ultimate vessel of possibility. In her, the world was given a new start.

"This January 1st, I would challenge you to...resolve to learn something from the woman we honor. Resolve to dwell in possibility. Resolve to see every day, not just this one, as a fresh beginning...Trust that God will see you through it—and then reflect on it in your heart. Just like Mary did."

My soul magnifies the Lord. (Luke 1:46)

Help me focus on new possibilities, Lord.

Also Available

We hope that you have enjoyed *Three Minutes a Day, Volume 48*. These other Christopher offerings may interest you:

- **News Notes** are published 10 times a year on a variety of topics of current interest. Single copies are free; quantity orders available.

- **Appointment Calendars** are suitable for wall or desk and provide an inspirational message for each day of the year.

- **DVDs** range from wholesome entertainment to serious discussions of family life and current social and spiritual issues.

- **Website—www.christophers.org**—has *Christopher Closeup* radio programs; links to our blog, Facebook and Twitter pages; a monthly *What's New* update; and much more.

For more information about The Christophers or to receive News Notes, please contact us:

The Christophers
5 Hanover Square
New York, NY 10004
Phone: 212-759-4050/888-298-4050
E-mail: mail@christophers.org
Website: www.christophers.org

The Christophers is a non-profit media organization founded in 1945 by Father James Keller, M.M. We share the message of personal responsibility and service to God and humanity with people of all faiths and no particular faith. Gifts are welcome and tax-deductible. Our legal title for wills is The Christophers, Inc.